THE HAIKI

משנת חיים

MISHNAS CHAYIM

VOLUME II

*Insights from the weekly Parshah
Illuminated by the Mishnah*

RABBI TZVI HEBEL

Published July, 2017

MISHNAS CHAYIM

© Copyright 2017 by Chevrah Lomdei Mishnah
(732) 364-7029 | www.ChevrahLomdeiMishnah.org

All rights reserved

No part of this book may be reproduced in any form, photocopying, or computer retrieval systems – even for personal use without written permission from the copyright holder, Chevrah Lomdei Mishnah, except by a reviewer who wishes to quote brief passages in connection with a review written for inclusion in magazines or newspapers.

The rights of the copyright holder will be strictly enforced.

ISBN: 978-1-944143-10-7

Author: Rabbi Tzvi Hebel
Editor: Mrs. Rivkah Schachnow
Design and Layout: Mrs. Raizy Flamm

*This volume is dedicated in memory of
my dear father*

Mr. Abraham Haikins

ר' אברהם יצחק ב"ר חיים צבי ע"ה, הכ"מ

נפטר כ"ו ניסן תשע"ז

*He believed in the success
of Chevrah Lomdei Mishnah
and constantly encouraged me
throughout its development and growth.
From its first baby steps,
he had faith in this endeavor
and the farsightedness to ensure
that what was just a possibility
would become reality.*

Haskamah of Harav Yeruchem Olshin, *shlita*,
for the first volume of *Mishnas Chayim*.

TRANSLATION of *Haskamah* of Harav Yeruchem Olshin, *shlita*, for the first volume of *Mishnas Chayim*.

יום ד' לפרשת קרח, סיון תשס"א

I was most gladdened to hear that my dear friend (*yedid*), the esteemed, precious Harav Tzvi Yehoshua Hebel, is progressing from strength to strength and is at the threshold of publishing his Torah insights on the weekly *parshiyos* in his valued *sefer*, *Mishnas Chayim*.

Harav Tzvi Yehoshua is a great Torah scholar (*talmid chacham*) who has toiled in Torah for many years in the great citadel of Torah, Bais Medrash Govoha of Lakewood. He is a true *ben aliyah*, adorned with the crown of greatness in Torah and with the crown of a good name, due to his exceptional character and pure fear of Heaven, which is a treasure house for his wisdom and for his Torah.

With the help of Hashem, he is exceptionally capable of offering original insights and clarifying difficult passages with tremendous clarity. His Torah insights are of a sweet and accurate quality, fit to be heard at the table of *talmidei chachamim*. He has already proven himself with his first important *sefer*, *The Neshamah Should Have an Aliyah*, in which he explained the subject matter very clearly and which was accepted with enthusiasm in the Torah world; as such, it has been of tremendous benefit to many people.

Rav Tzvi Yehoshua is also a disseminator of Torah to young students, and he has succeeded greatly in raising their levels of Torah and *yiras Shamayim*. Now, he has merited, with the help of Hashem, to produce this wonderful work, which was written in English to be of greatest benefit to the general public. His insights are based upon the strong foundations of the teachings of the *gedolei hador* and are comprised of words that emanate from a pure heart, full of a love of Torah and a love and fear of Hashem. Certainly these words will enter the hearts of those who learn this *sefer*, bringing those who study it close to Hashem and His Torah.

I hereby bless my precious *yedid* that his *sefer* should be accepted wholeheartedly, and he should merit to continue rising higher and higher in levels of Torah study and fear of Hashem, until he becomes like one of the *gedolei* Torah. May he merit to learn and to teach in a state of tranquility, with peace of mind and happiness and pleasure from his esteemed family. May he merit reveal many Torah insights and to author many important works for the benefit of the public and to disseminate Torah and fear of Heaven among the Jewish people.

Who writes and signs for the honor of Torah, those who toil in it and disseminate it,

(Harav) Yeruchem Olshin

לזכר ולעילוי נשמות

ר' חיים צבי ב"ר אברהם יצחק ע"ה

פיגא ריזא בת ר' ברוך שלום ע"ה

ציפא רבקה בת ר' ברוך ע"ה

ברוך ב"ר משה ע"ה

חנה מירא בת ר' שלמה ע"ה

Provide eternal merit through Mishnah study

RABBI MOSHE HAIKINS | FOUNDER AND PRESIDENT

25 Tammuz, 5777

It is with great pleasure that Chevrah Lomdei Mishnah presents you, dear reader, with a second volume of Mishnas Chayim, a digest of weekly *divrei Torah* on the *parshah*, seen through the lens of the Mishnah. This project of Chevrah Lomdei Mishnah has been enjoyed by many (in both the hard copy and email versions), who appreciate the interesting and varied Torah thoughts written by my dear friend and colleague, Rabbi Tzvi Hebel. His clear, carefully crafted messages, which display a deep understanding of Torah, as well as his witty observations, are what draw readers to these words of wisdom week after week.

Today, you can enjoy Mishnas Chayim weekly via email or by visiting our website.

As the new calendar year of 5778 approaches, with it begins a new Torah-reading cycle. Chevrah Lomdei Mishnah hopes that you will be inspired throughout the year by these *divrei Torah*, as you read – or rather – study, learn, incorporate and internalize its messages.

To our great sorrow, my father, Mr. Abraham Haikins, ר' אברהם יצחק ב"ר חיים צבי ע"ה הכ"מ, passed away a mere few months ago, on 26 Nissan 5777. It is my honor to dedicate this volume in his merit.

Since its inception twelve years ago, Chevrah Lomdei Mishnah has become the premier organization for helping Jews around the world provide eternal merit for their departed loved ones. Since that time, we have expanded our scope to become a leading source in raising awareness of how to provide merit for the departed, as well as in offering words of solace for those who have suffered the loss of a loved one. Visit our site at **www.ChevrahLomdeiMishnah.org** for a full list of opportunities and materials.

Wishing you all a year of learning and inspiration,

Rabbi Moshe Haikins
Founder and President
Chevrah Lomdei Mishnah/The Society for Mishnah Study

40 East Thirteenth Street, Lakewood, NJ 08701 | TEL 732.364.7029 | FAX 732.364.8386 | ChevrahLomdeiMishnah.org

Table of Contents

SEFER BEREISHIS 5

BEREISHIS............................	The Dawn of Time: What Was on the Menu?	7
NO'ACH................................	Feed the Animals	11
LECH LECHA......................	Yetzer Hara: The Dastardly Destroyer	15
VAYEIRA..............................	The Incredible Life of Yitzchak Avinu	19
CHAYEI SARAH.................	Dinnertime Deferment	23
TOLDOS	The View from Above	27
VAYEITZEI..........................	Share the Wealth	31
VAYISHLACH	The Instruction Manual for Galus (Exile)	35
VAYEISHEV	Origin of the Blood Libel..	39
MIKEITZ	The Royalty of the Chashmona'im	43
VAYIGASH...........................	On That Day	47
VAYECHI.............................	The Fate of the Ten Lost Tribes of Yisrael...........................	51

SEFER SHEMOS 53

SHEMOS...............................	Out-Scheming the Schemer	57
VA'EIRA	Honored Pharaoh	61
BO	The Egyptian House of Horrors..	65
BESHALACH	Timely Justice	69
YISRO...................................	Privileged Information..	73
MISHPATIM........................	Every Dog Has His (Sabbath) Day	77
TERUMAH	Who are the Leviim?	81
TETZAVEH	A Fitting Crown	85
KI SISA.................................	The Thin Line	89
VAYAKHEL..........................	Plenty of Room	93
PEKUDEI.............................	A Mountain on Top of a Hair...	99

SEFER VAYIKRA 101

VAYIKRA .... *The "Kuntz" of Being Humble* 103
TZAV .... *Relating to Children – at the Seder* 107
SHEMINI .... *Silence – Not Always Golden* 111
TAZRIA-METZORA .... *Bringing Down the House* 115
ACHAREI MOS-KEDOSHIM ..... *The Logic Behind Wonders* 119
EMOR .... *Praying for Rain* 123
BEHAR-BECHUKOSAI .... *How Can You Sleep at Night?* 127

SEFER BAMIDBAR 131

BAMIDBAR .... *Grass and Torah* 133
NASSO .... *Under the Influence* 137
BEHA'ALOSECHA .... *It Can Happen to the Best of Us* 141
SHELACH .... *Warning: Flammable!* 145
KORACH .... *Where in the World...?* 149
CHUKAS .... *The Complete Cow* 153
BALAK .... *Bilam and* (L'havdil Elef v'alfei Havdalos) *R' Yose ben Kisma* 157
PINCHAS .... *Pinchas and Zimri: The Ironic Climax* 161
MATOS-MASEI .... *Secrets of Masei* 165

SEFER DEVARIM 169

DEVARIM ... *Re-examining the Churban: What Happened to the Beis Hamikdash?* 171
VA'ESCHANAN .... *The Third Beis Hamikdash* 175
EIKEV .... *The Hands of Moshe* 179
RE'EH .... *No Retirement* 183
SHOFTIM .... *Men and Trees* 187
KI SEITZEI .... *A Joyous Breakdown* 191
KI SAVO .... *Fuel for Flight* 195
NITZAVIM .... *Take Up Your Weapons* 199
VAYEILECH .... *The Final Surge* 203
HA'AZINU .... *Tishrei: The Big Picture* 207

SEFER BEREISHIS
ספר בראשית

לזכר ולעילוי נשמות
אסתר בת צבי הערש ע"ה
נתן שלום ע"ה **בן יהודה הכהן** נ"י

BEREISHIS

The Dawn of Time: What Was on the Menu?

THESE DAYS WHEN DIETING IS ALL THE RAGE, SOME may want to point to Adam Harishon as the pioneer of vegetarians. Such a notion does seem to be supported by the plain reading of the section in this week's *parshah* in which Adam is informed of his fare; as the verse states (*Bereishis 1:29-30*): "Behold, I have given you all herbaceous growth... on the face of the earth, and... fruit of the tree... they shall be to you for consumption. And to all animals of the earth, and all birds of the heavens, and all that crawls on the land... all vegetation (has been designated) for consumption." The picture certainly appears to be one of a world wherein all creatures – from the lowliest worm to human beings – share a vegetarian lifestyle.

Adam Harishon – Vegetarian?

A closer look reveals that the matter may not be so simple. Consider the prohibition of *eiver min hachai*, which forbids the

---

KINDLY TAKE A MOMENT TO STUDY **MISHNAS CHAYIM** IN THE MERIT OF
HILDA BAS TZVI HYMAN A"H
A FELLOW JEW WHO PASSED AWAY WITH NO RELATIVES TO ARRANGE TORAH STUDY ON BEHALF OF HER *NESHAMAH*

consumption of a limb separated from a live animal. *Eiver min hachai* is included in the list of the seven pre-Sinaitic laws, which the Gemara (*Sanhedrin 56b*) derives from a command Hashem issues to Adam in this week's *parshah* (*Bereishis 2:16*). Now, if Adam was already proscribed from all manner of meat-consumption, what need was there for a further directive singling out *eiver min hachai*? The obvious implication seems to be that regular meat-consumption was, indeed, an option for Adam Harishon (*cf. Tosafos, ibid., s.v. Achol*).

Perhaps even more blatant is Chazal's depiction of the idyllic life afforded to Adam in Gan Eden (*Avos D'Rebbi Nassan 1:8*). They describe him reclining in the Garden, waited upon by angelic attendants who would roast meat for him and prepare his wine. (This situation continued until it was noticed by a snake with a propensity to envy. From that point on matters proceeded steadily downhill.) In any event, the description hardly fits one of a purely vegetarian lifestyle. And so we are saddled with an apparent incongruity: was Adam a vegetarian, or wasn't he?

Different Types, Different Times, Different Methods

ON THIS ISSUE, VARIOUS SAGES OF THE TOSAFIST school advance differing approaches. The *Chizkuni* (*Bereishis 1:29*) implies that Adam's menu was, indeed, restricted to vegetarian dishes. The meat prepared for him by the angels was of a different sort altogether, as it descended from Heaven (*cf. Sanhedrin 59b*). As such, this meal did not have actual "meat" status – insofar as the general ban on eating flesh was concerned (one could contemplate whether it could be cooked in a *milchige* pot, eaten during the Nine Days, etc.).

The *Tosafos al Hatorah* take a different tack. While seeming to confer "*fleishige*" status on all types of meat (regardless of origin), a distinction is drawn between varying periods of time. They contend that while Adam was proscribed from eating all manner of meat, this ban was instituted only *after* the sin of eating from the

Tree of Knowledge. As long as he still resided in Gan Eden, meat dishes were permissible, and so Adam could partake there of the angels' offerings.

A final approach is offered by *Tosafos* to Sanhedrin (*56b*). They differentiate not in origin or time-periods, but in the method of procurement. According to this view, the ban applies only to the killing of animals for their meat; but the flesh of animals that died on their own (or prepared by celestial chefs) was permissible to Adam. This accounts for the specific directive prohibiting *eiver min hachai*: since regular meat (of an expired animal) was permissible, one would assume that the same would be true of a limb that fell (on its own) from a live animal. It was such an entity that the Torah sought to restrict.

To sum up, then, it appears that we have three views as to Adam's status as a vegetarian: According to the *Chizkuni*, it seems that Adam could only eat foods of non-meat status; the *Tosafos al Hatorah* contend that Adam became a vegetarian only after the sin of Gan Eden; and according to *Tosafos* in Sanhedrin, Adam was a full-fledged meat eater, restricted only from killing for his food.

Strange Bedfellows

A FINAL POINT RELEVANT TO THE TOPIC IS THE implication of the blessing Hashem conferred upon Adam. In the verse immediately preceding the ones discussed above, Hashem declares (*v. 28*): "And you shall rule over the fish of the sea and the birds of the sky and all of the animals..." What manner of dominance would man exert over the animals? It could very well take the form of labor, as he impresses the ox and the horse into agricultural service. However, what productive farm work or transportation could be provided by *fish*? The verse seems to be stating that for Adam Harishon, there is a permissible form of trapping animals for food – namely, fishing! This seems to lend some support to the notion that Adam was, in fact, a flesh-eater.

The Gemara itself (*Sanhedrin 59b*) clarifies the issue, explaining that the intent of the verse – even with regard to fish – is for labor and not as a food source. How could this be possible? The Gemara illustrates based on the law prohibiting the enlistment of two different types of animals in work, as the verse states: "You shall not plow with an ox and a donkey together" (*Devarim 22:10*). Although the *passuk* mentions ox and donkey, the prohibition actually applies to any two (different) animals paired together, a fact reflected in the following Mishnah (*Kilayim 8:2*):

בְּהֵמָה עִם בְּהֵמָה וְחַיָּה עִם חַיָּה, בְּהֵמָה עִם חַיָּה... אֲסוּרִין לַחֲרֹשׁ וְלִמְשֹׁךְ וּלְהַנְהִיג.

"Of the following combinations – any domesticated animal with another (type of) domesticated animal; any wild animal with another (type of) wild animal; a domesticated animal with a wild animal... – one is forbidden to employ them in plowing, pulling or leading."

In any event, the aforementioned Gemara cites the sage Rachvah, who posed quite an interesting query on this issue. Rachvah wondered if the prohibition would apply when one hitches up his wagon in the following way: part of the reins are attached to a goat who travels on land, while the other section is strapped to a fish who pulls it in the water. Regardless of the conclusion reached in Rachvah's question, we do see a manifestation of the harnessing of "fish-power" for productive use. As such, the exhortation to Adam to dominate the fish of the sea can be understood in the sense of subjugation to labor. Thus, the prohibition to kill for flesh remained intact. (It was not lifted until after the flood, as elaborated on in *Mishnas Chayim, parshas No'ach, 5772*).

לזכר ולעילוי נשמת
אביגדור יעקב ע"ה בן אזניק נ"י

NO'ACH

Feed the Animals

HAVING FOCUSED LAST WEEK ON THE TOPIC OF THE dining options of Adam Harishon, we turn now to a similar issue pertaining to this week's *parshah*: namely, the endeavor of feeding the inhabitants of No'ach's *teivah* (ark).

While appearing initially straightforward, the *passuk* that addresses the subject, upon closer examination, actually raises some significant perplexities. Hashem instructs No'ach to prepare sustenance for the duration of the upcoming flood:

וְאַתָּה קַח־לְךָ מִכָּל־מַאֲכָל... וְאָסַפְתָּ אֵלֶיךָ וְהָיָה לְךָ וְלָהֶם לְאָכְלָה.

"And you, take for you from all food... and gather it to you, and it will be for you and for them to eat" (Bereishis 6:21-22).

What seems most puzzling about the wording of the *passuk* is that it seems to contain several superfluities. Right at the beginning, we encounter repetition: "And you, take for **you**." Furthermore, an entire phrase here appears completely unnecessary. After telling

---

Kindly take a moment to study **Mishnas Chayim** in the merit of
Roy ben Tzvi Ya'akov A"H
a fellow Jew who passed away with no relatives to arrange Torah study on behalf of his *neshamah*

No'ach to procure food, why must he be told "that it will be for you and for them to eat." After all, isn't that kind of the point of food?

BUT PERHAPS THE GREATEST ISSUE TO BE RAISED here is the question of logistics. For those who appreciate thrilling, wondrous sights, one of the most remarkable spectacles to behold is feeding time at the hippo exhibit in the Biblical Zoo in Yerushalayim. Summoned by the keeper at mealtime, the hippos approach, their huge mouths agape. The keeper lifts a watermelon or two into the air, and then hurls it towards the cavernous openings. The hippos' great jaws come crashing down, a gush of pink spray spewing forth from between them. This is followed by a few buckets-full of cucumbers, any number of heads of lettuce and a plethora of other vegetables. By the time the exercise is complete, what basically amounts to the contents of the entire produce section at the local supermarket has been emptied into the animals' gullets.

Bon Apetít

And this is just *one* meal for *one or two* animals. Bear in mind that the *teivah* was to house every single living species of the entire animal kingdom (excluding fish). Furthermore, it was not just one day for which No'ach had to provide. He had to store enough provisions to last throughout their sojourn in the *teivah*, the duration of which is recorded in the Mishnah in Eduyos (*2:10*):

מִשְׁפַּט דּוֹר הַמַּבּוּל, שְׁנֵים עָשָׂר חֹדֶשׁ.

"*The Flood spanned a twelve-month period.*"

This means, of course, that No'ach had to bring enough to feed every single one of earth's creatures for an entire year. How could he possibly gather such a gargantuan pile of provisions, and where, pray tell, was he supposed to put this astronomical volume of (perishable) supplies in a *teivah* of limited size, already packed with doubles (at least) of every creature that existed in the world?

Obviously, miraculous intervention was necessary. R' Yehonasan Eibshitz (*Tiferes Yehonasan*) describes the nature and mechanics of this wondrous contingency, at the same time shedding much light on the proper understanding of the *passuk*.

A Little Planning Can Go a Long Way...

MIRACLES, BY DEFINITION, ARE INHERENTLY supernatural; nevertheless, we do find that Hashem employs certain guiding principles in performing them. While He is the Omnipotent One, capable of any feat, it appears that Hashem exercised His ability to fashion something "*yeish mei'ayin*" (literally out of thin air) only at the beginning of the creation of the world. Since then, He deals mainly with "*yeish mi'yeish*" (making something out of pre-existing material).

Consider the miracle wrought through the prophet Elisha on behalf of the destitute widow (*Melachim II 4:1-7*). The woman had been in danger of losing her children, as the hardhearted creditor threatened to seize and impress them into servitude to satisfy an unpaid loan. Elisha provided the solution to her quandary. He instructed her to take her sole possession – a single container of oil – and empty its contents into another vessel. She did so, and – lo and behold – while the new vessel was filled, the old one had not emptied. She again poured the contents into another vessel, with the same result; new oil was yielded, while the original stock had not depleted. She repeated this exercise a number of times, filling many vessels. She was then able to sell this windfall of new oil and pay off the creditor.

It is noteworthy that the oil did not simply appear from nowhere; it was necessary to begin with a base of pre-existing matter, from which new oil was miraculously generated (*cf. Mishnas Chayim, Vayeishev, 5770*).

The same principle, explains R' Yehonasan, was manifest in No'ach's pre-flood preparations. And this is apparent from the *passuk*. Looking carefully, we see that Hashem actually instructed No'ach to procure enough food *just for himself* – "You, take **for you**." It was certainly possible to gather and store this limited

No'ach / 13

volume. But this, Hashem assured him, would be the "base" from which the animals' provisions would generate upon demand.

This accounts for the *passuk*'s repetition. Hashem first instructed No'ach to gather food: "Take for you from all food." But, as mentioned, this was No'ach's personal store. How was he to provide for the animals? The *passuk* continues: "It will be for you **and for them** to eat." Far from superfluous information, Hashem was relating to No'ach something eye-opening indeed: He need not be concerned for the animals' welfare, for their needs would be amply supplied. And the supply would come from No'ach's own provisions, through Hashem's wondrous, guiding hand.

The *passuk* goes on to relate No'ach's compliance: "And No'ach did all that Hashem commanded him." At first glance, this also seems unnecessary; is it "news" that No'ach did as he was told? In light of his approach, R' Yehonasan explains that the verse is in fact relaying No'ach's praise. He was about to embark on a major undertaking, which could only be successful through miraculous intervention. But No'ach trusted in Hashem and faithfully fulfilled His command.

לזכר ולעילוי נשמת
רב משה בן יצחק אשר הי"ד

LECH LECHA

Yetzer Hara: The Dastardly Destroyer

KNOWING HOW THE YETZER HARA (EVIL Inclination) operates is not only informative, but a crucial and effective tool in protecting ourselves, as well. The more we are aware of his strategies and methods, the better chance we will have in avoiding his pitfalls.

A FAVORITE PLOY OF THE YETZER HARA IS ON display in this week's *parshah*, with Avraham's nephew Lot providing a prime illustration. When the time came to separate from Avraham, Lot's choice of relocation was "interesting," to say the least. "And Lot lifted up his eyes, and he saw the entire plain of the Yarden, that it was fertile ground; (this was) before Hashem destroyed Sodom and Amorah. It was like the Garden of Hashem... And Lot chose (this location) for himself..." (*Bereishis 13:10,11*). This was the area in which the sinful city of Sodom was located. The *passuk* continues, describing Lot's journey to his new home: "And Lot

From Riches to Rags

Kindly take a moment to study Mishnas Chayim in the merit of

Esther bas Eizik a"h

a fellow Jew who passed away with no relatives to arrange Torah study on behalf of her *neshamah*

traveled *mikedem*." While the simple meaning of this term is "from the east," Rashi comments homiletically that it reveals Lot's true mindset: he moved away from the **Kadmon**o Shel Olam (Hashem, the "Ancient" One of the World, Who has always existed). "I am no longer interested – not in Avraham nor his G-d," Lot declared.

From his associations with Avraham, Lot emerged as a very wealthy man. "And also to Lot, who journeyed with Avraham, were sheep, cattle and tents" (*ibid. v. 5*). He then settled in a luxuriant, fertile area and even rose to prominence among his new townsfolk, obtaining a judgeship (*Rashi on 19:1*). Thus, at the same time that he reached the pinnacle of material success, he became distant from his Creator.

Fast forward to the end of the story. In *parshas* Vayeira, the city of sin is obliterated. Lot – in the merit of his righteous uncle – is spared. But his situation at that point contrasts markedly with the picture of grandeur in this week's *parshah*. At the end, he is told, "Flee with your life" (*19:17*) – about the only thing remaining to him. He had to abandon his possessions, his neighborhood went up in smoke, he lost most of his family, and his new home was a cave.

The entire episode is markedly similar to the description in the Mishnah in Avos (*4:9*):

> רַבִּי יוֹנָתָן אוֹמֵר, כָּל הַמְקַיֵּם אֶת הַתּוֹרָה מֵעֹנִי, סוֹפוֹ לְקַיְּמָהּ מֵעֹשֶׁר. וְכָל הַמְבַטֵּל אֶת הַתּוֹרָה מֵעֹשֶׁר, סוֹפוֹ לְבַטְּלָהּ מֵעֹנִי.

> "R' Yonasan says: Whoever fulfills the Torah from a state of poverty – will in the end fulfill it from a state of wealth. And whoever neglects the Torah from wealth – will in the end neglect it from poverty."

The Post-Mortem

WHAT HAPPENED HERE? LOT SEEMS TO HAVE started off alright, his association with Avraham benefitting him spiritually and materially. But when he veered off the path, everything spiraled completely downhill.

The Chafetz Chaim (*Nefutzos Yisrael*, ch. 3) dissects for us what was really happening behind the scenes, revealing the Satan hard at work.

He begins his explanation with an illustrative story: A wealthy magnate, in need of assistance in keeping track of his business affairs, sought to hire a qualified bookkeeper. This was perfect for Chaim, skilled in this area, who was desperate for a source of livelihood. Thus he came into the employ of the magnate, who offered him $100 per month, a princely sum in those days.

But Chaim had an erstwhile enemy, a hateful and devious man. As soon as he got wind of Chaim's newfound arrangement, he sprang into action.

The schemer approached the magnate with a proposition. "I know," he told him, "that you own much real estate and could really be earning a huge sum from tenants. But I also know the problem – you can't find a capable landlord to handle the rent collection. So I have the perfect solution for you, as I know just the man for the job. If you hire Chaim for this endeavor, the profits will start rolling in."

The businessman had to admit that the proposal was sound. So he summoned Chaim and informed him of the new terms of his employment. "It turns out," he explained, "that I don't really need you so much for bookkeeping; I can really handle that angle myself. What I really need you to do for me is ensure that my tenants pay their rents. Unfortunately, that type of work carries a salary of only $20 a month, but it is still steady pay." Chaim, in his destitute state, was in no position to turn down the offer. So he swallowed the pay cut.

And so things continued for a year or so. But Chaim's enemy was still not placated, knowing that Chaim still had work – at his own behest, no less. So he contrived any number of accusations of Chaim's delinquency, reporting regularly to the magnate. Eventually, his employment was terminated completely, and Chaim was left with nothing.

This, explains the Chafetz Chaim, is the Yetzer Hara's diabolical plan, which played itself out in the case of Lot. The Yetzer Hara sets his eyes on a servant of Hashem, begrudging him the inestimable reward that awaits him in the World to Come. With an aim toward eliminating this eternal bounty, he arranges for an "employment adjustment" of sorts. This often comes in the form of newfound material wealth, as the Yetzer Hara entices his target to devote more and more time and energy to its pursuit – at the expense of his spiritual endeavors.

But even when the Yetzer Hara is successful in his goals, he is not content. He might have wiped out his victim's store of reward in the World to Come – but he has left him with considerable fruits in This World! Thus, he gets back to work, engaged both in enticement to more sin and with subsequent *kitrugim* (accusations) in the Heavenly lair. This continues until, eventually, the hapless victim, ensnared in his trap, ends up without Olam Haba (the World to Come) or Olam Hazeh (This World).

"*Sofo l'vatlah mei'oni*" – in the end, he will be neglecting Torah from a state of poverty. May Hashem protect us!

לזכר ולעילוי נשמות
אריה אשר בן זאב הכהן ע"ה
גיטל בת יצחק הלוי ע"ה

VAYEIRA

The Incredible Life of Yitzchak Avinu

The very familiar episode of *Akeidas Yitzchak* (Binding of Yitzchak) takes place in this week's *parshah*. What may be less well-known, however, is Yitzchak's fate in the wake of this event.

MOST PEOPLE, PERHAPS, CAN SUPPLY A BASIC rundown of the story, which would likely read something like this: Hashem presents Avraham with the ultimate trial, bidding him to offer his beloved son as a sacrifice. Avraham endeavors to fulfill the command, taking Yitzchak to Mt. Moriah and binding him on the altar (to prevent movement). As Avraham lifts the knife to perform the slaughter, Yitzchak is granted a last-minute reprieve. An angel of Hashem calls out to Avraham, stops the act and informs the patriarch that he has proven his devotion. A ram is discovered and sacrificed in Yitzchak's stead, and father and son return happily home.

All's Well that Ends Well...

KINDLY TAKE A MOMENT TO STUDY **MISHNAS CHAYIM** IN THE MERIT OF
TZIPPA BAS **YA'AKOV** A"H
A FELLOW JEW WHO PASSED AWAY WITH NO RELATIVES TO ARRANGE TORAH STUDY ON BEHALF OF HER NESHAMAH

With one possible exception, the details above are pretty accurate. As we shall see, the ending may not have occurred in the exact fashion just mentioned.

The same observation can be applied to a Mishnah in Ta'anis, which discusses the elongated prayers offered on certain fast days. The Mishnah (2:4) discusses the first of these elaborations:

עַל הָרִאשׁוֹנָה הוּא אוֹמֵר, מִי שֶׁעָנָה אֶת אַבְרָהָם בְּהַר הַמּוֹרִיָּה, הוּא יַעֲנֶה אֶתְכֶם וְיִשְׁמַע בְּקוֹל צַעֲקַתְכֶם הַיּוֹם הַזֶּה, בָּרוּךְ אַתָּה ה' גּוֹאֵל יִשְׂרָאֵל.

"For the first (expanded blessing of the Shemoneh Esrei), he recites the following: 'The One Who answered Avraham at Mt. Moriah – may He answer you today and hearken to the voice of your cry. Blessed are You, Hashem, the Redeemer of Yisrael.'"

This Mishnah alludes to the fact that Avraham was "answered" at the time and place of the *Akeidah*, referring presumably to the fact that his son Yitzchak was spared. While the Maharsha (*Ta'anis 15a*) may have had a bit of a different take on this point, it certainly does appear that this was the Yerushalmi's understanding of the Mishnah. We see this from its questioning of the the blessing's conclusion, asking why the blessing ends with "Redeemer of Yisrael" instead of "Redeemer of Yitzchak." (The Yerushalmi proceeds to answer that Yitzchak's deliverance constituted salvation for all of Yisrael, his progeny.) Yet here again, as we shall see, the matter may be up for discussion: Was Yitzchak in fact "saved"?

The first apparent deviation from the "conventional" version of events comes from a statement in the Medrash. In Pirkei D'R'Eliezer (*ch. 31*), R' Yehudah asserts that Yitzchak actually expired during the proceedings: "As soon as the blade was about to make contact with Yitzchak's neck, his soul exited his body." (The same phrase is used in reference to the experience of Klal Yisrael at Har Sinai, when their souls left their bodies from fright. They were subsequently resurrected).

However, this statement alone does not present a real conflict with our understanding of the *Akeidah* and its aftermath. For as the Medrash continues, the issue was immediately rectified: "When the call emanated from the Heavens, 'Do not send your hand against the lad' (*Bereishis 22:12*), his soul re-entered his body, he was untied and stood on his feet... and recited the blessing, 'Blessed are You, Hashem, Who resurrects the dead.'"

But then we come to the amazing comments of the Megaleh Amukos, venerated Kabbalistic sage of the seventeenth century.

The Missing Years

IN NEXT WEEK'S *PARSHAH*, WHICH BEGINS WITH THE sad tidings of the passing of Sarah Imeinu, the *passuk* relates how "Avraham came to eulogize Sarah and cry over her" (*ibid. 23:2*). Where was Yitzchak during this whole episode? He doesn't appear in the entire narrative relating to the mourning practices for Sarah. Seemingly, it would have been appropriate for Yitzchak to take part in the ceremonies for his own mother!

The Megaleh Amukos (*parshas Chayei Sarah*) answers with a stark revelation that he bases upon Chazal: Yitzchak was not present for Sarah's eulogy because, at the time, *he also was no longer among the living.* He was residing in Gan Eden, where he remained for a few years.

With this, the Megaleh Amukos resolves a fascinating mathematical issue that arises in the teachings of Chazal. The Gemara tells us (*Pesachim 94b*) that a (theoretical) journey from earth to the "*rakiya*" (firmament) would take 500 years. The Medrash finds an allusion to this phenomenon in the *passuk* from *Keriyas Shema*: "So that your days be numerous... on the land that Hashem swore to your forefathers... like the days of the heavens on the earth" (*Devarim 11:21*). The Medrash renders: The days of the forefathers are equal to the span of the heavens above the earth. That is, the travel distance (in years) to reach the heavens from earth is equal to the sum total of the lifespans of the three *Avos* (patriarchs) – namely, 500 years.

However, asserts the Megaleh Amukos, something doesn't "add up" here. Avraham lived 175 years; Yitzchak, 180; and Ya'akov, 147. The total comes to 502, not 500!

Based on the above regarding *Akeidas Yitzchak*, however, the equation is indeed sound. The Megaleh Amukos explains that, post-*Akeidah*, Yitzchak remained in Gan Eden for two years. These two years during which he literally resided "over" and outside of the astronomical stratosphere are not to be included in the count of "earth years." Thus, minus these two "extra-terrestrial" years, the *Avos* did, in fact, live a combined total of exactly 500 years, in line with the calculation of the Medrash.

In any event, the eye-opening information supplied by the Megaleh Amukos does not necessarily contradict the Yerushalmi's understanding that Yitzchak was in fact "redeemed." For even according to the Megaleh Amukos, Yitzchak did return to earth, whereupon he married Rivkah. This is also the meaning of Rashi's comment to the enigmatic description of Rivkah falling from her camel upon first laying eyes on her prospective husband (*Bereishis 24:44*). What caused her to swoon? Rashi there states: "She saw that he was '*mehudar*' (glorious). What does that mean, exactly? The Megaleh Amukos attributes the awesome radiance of his appearance to the fact that he had just returned from the ethereal realm of Gan Eden.

לזכר ולעילוי נשמות
אריה ליב בן צבי הירש ע״ה
שרה חיה בת ישראל ע״ה

CHAYEI SARAH

Dinnertime Deferment

THIS WEEK'S *PARSHAH* RELATES THE PLEASANT narrative of Rivkah's display of altruistic kindness. Seeking a suitable wife for his master's son, Eliezer the servant of Avraham arranges a test of sorts: He will ask for a drink from the water-drawing maidens, and whoever agrees and offers water to his camels as well will have proven herself to be the prospective bride. And so it plays out when Rivkah approaches. Eliezer asks for water, and Rivkah generously responds, giving him to drink and filling the trough for his camels, as well.

Nothing untoward here, right?

ACTUALLY, IT MIGHT NOT BE SO SIMPLE – especially in light of a *halachah* emerging from a *passuk* found in *Keriyas Shema*. The verse states: "And I will supply grass in your field for your animals, and you will eat and be satiated" (*Devarim 11:15*). The Gemara (*Berachos 40a*) notes that the order in the *passuk* is quite deliberate: First – "And I will supply grass... for your animals," and only then

Camels First?

Kindly take a moment to study **Mishnas Chayim** in the merit of
Binyomin *ben* Ya'akov *a"h*
a fellow Jew who passed away with no relatives to arrange Torah study on behalf of his *neshamah*

"you shall eat." From this inference, the Gemara concludes: "It is forbidden for a person to dine before he feeds his animal."

Thus, Rivkah's actions may need to be reexamined. "And she said: 'Drink, my master'... And she finished giving him to drink, and she said, 'I will also draw (water) for your camels'... And she drew (water) for all his camels" (*Bereishis 24:18-20*). Thus we see that she *first* gave water to Eliezer and only supplied his camels when he was finished drinking! Was this a laudable good deed or a contravention of *halachah*?

The Machatzis Hashekel (*Orach Chaim 167:18*) states unequivocally that the fact that the Torah recorded the deed of our righteous matriarch means that not only was it permissible, but that we should learn from and duplicate it. Regarding the apparent contradiction (to the prohibition against eating before the animals), he concurs with the resolution provided by the Sefer Chassidim, who draws the following distinction. The above *halachah* was stated specifically with regard to *eating*; in that case, one must ensure that his animals are served first. Drinking, however, is another matter, as we see from the episode with Rivkah. When it comes to drinking, we need not give precedence to the beasts.

A number of commentators, however, take issue with this attempt to differentiate between eating and drinking in this matter. Why, exactly, should there be such a difference in the first place? Furthermore, they point out that the assertion of the Sefer Chassidim seems to be at odds with the Gemara elsewhere. The same statement (prohibiting eating before feeding the animals) appears in the Gemara in Gittin (*62a*), but with a "twist." The wording there states: "It is forbidden *litom* (to taste) before feeding one's animal." Things may have squared with the terminology in Berachos, which spoke of a prohibition *l'echol* (to eat); there's room to infer that the rule is limited just to solids and not liquids. But this distinction seems not to pass muster with the "*litom*" version of Gittin, as "tasting" applies equally to eating or drinking.

The Ohr Hachaim Hakadosh (*Bereishis 24:19*) formulates a different distinction. The issue is not eating vs. drinking; rather, the matter revolves around urgency. Under normal circumstances, one must give precedence to serving the animals first, regardless of the substance of the offerings. To this was the Gemara in Berachos referring. But Eliezer was a special case; having traveled from afar, his thirst was quite strong, and he suffered substantial discomfort. In cases of extreme need or danger, we tend first to the person – as evidenced by Rivkah's deed.

But there seems to be room to raise questions on this explanation as well. The assumption here is that Eliezer was in "great need" of a drink. But is that necessarily the case? Seemingly, Eliezer was a capable individual who could readily have helped himself; the whole arrangement with the water-drawers was but a contrived exercise for matrimonial purposes. It might be that Eliezer wasn't so desperate for a drink after all.

Polly Want a Cracker – Now

AN ALTERNATE EXPLANATION – ONE UNAFFECTED by the points raised above – is offered by the Chasam Sofer (cited in *Shailos U'teshuvos K'sav Sofer, Orach Chaim §22*). He provides yet another distinction, one that appears sporadically in Shas, such as in the laws of feeding animals on Shabbos. The Mishnah (*Shabbos 24:3*) states:

אֵין נוֹתְנִין מַיִם לִפְנֵי דְבוֹרִים וְלִפְנֵי יוֹנִים שֶׁבַּשּׁוֹבָךְ, אֲבָל נוֹתְנִין לִפְנֵי אֲוָזִים וְתַרְנְגוֹלִים וְלִפְנֵי יוֹנֵי הַרְדְּסִיּוֹת.

> "One may not place water (on Shabbos) before bees or doves of the cote. But one may place it before geese, chickens and Herodian doves."

Why is it forbidden to lay out water for one class of creatures and permissible for the others? The Gemara (*Shabbos 155b*) attributes the difference to their ability to procure their own food. For those creatures that can forage for themselves, it is unnecessary to give them food; hence one is prohibited from providing them their needs on Shabbos. Regarding the others, they are considered to be in a state of *"mezonosan alecha"* – they depend on their human owners for their sustenance. As such, one may put out their rations on Shabbos.

Chayei Sarah / 25

This same distinction, explains the Chasam Sofer, is the determining factor in our discussion as well. The Gemara forbids one to eat before feeding the animals – but which ones? Those characterized as *"mezonosan alecha,"* that is, *his own* animals, who rely upon him for their nourishment. Thus, the halachah was totally non-applicable in the case of Rivkah – because they were not her camels but Eliezer's. Additionally, the matter follows the giver; thus, once Rivkah was authorized to offer Eliezer first, there was no issue with him partaking before his camels.

An interesting practical ramification emerges from this approach. Someone who owns a pet bird, for example, must first see to it that his bird is given food before he himself has his morning meal. But if the same individual has guests staying with him – on whom the bird is not dependent – the host can serve them their scrambled eggs before taking care of Polly the parakeet. Then, after guests and bird are provided for, he can join them for breakfast (*Piskei Teshuvos 167:15*).

לזכר ולעילוי נשמת
שמואל אליעזר בן נפתלי ע"ה

TOLDOS

The View from Above

IN THIS WEEK'S *PARSHAH*, THE TORAH PROVIDES A description of Yitzchak having reached an advanced age: "And it was, as Yitzchak grew old, and the vision of his eyes was weak" (*Bereishis 27:1*). Seemingly, his weakened eyesight was a result of the deterioration of old age.

HOWEVER, RASHI EXPLAINS DIFFERENTLY. THE Torah's mentioning that he grew old was the setting for the upcoming episode and the reason he prepared to bless his son. But (as the Netziv points out in Ha'amek Davar), the *passuk* itself never stated explicitly that his old age was the *cause* of his vision impairment.

Malachim (Angels) Don't Need Glasses

So what caused it? Rashi cites the Medrash that this condition was occasioned by an earlier event – the *Akeidah* (Binding of Yitzchak):

"... Yitzchak was bound upon the altar, and his father sought to slaughter him (in fulfillment of Hashem's command, which was a

---

Kindly take a moment to study **Mishnas Chayim** in the merit of
Yonah ben Reuven A"H
a fellow Jew who passed away with no relatives to arrange Torah study on behalf of his *neshamah*

trial for Avraham). At that moment, the Heavens parted, and the ministering angels beheld the scene. They began to cry, and their tears fell into Yitzchak's eyes. That is how his eyesight was dimmed."

Elsewhere (*Mishnas Chayim, parshas Kedoshim, 5770*), we examined this Medrash, focusing on the underlying causes of the angels' tears: why, indeed, did they cry? Surely, as celestial beings privy to the broader picture, they must have known about the magnitude of this event and the tremendous benefit that would accrue to Klal Yisrael for generations to come as a result. Instead of weeping, they should have rejoiced! We now approach the Medrash from a slightly different angle – but may uncover, in the process, further clarification of the issue of the angels' tears.

What is particularly noteworthy in this narrative is the reference to the opening of the skies: "At that moment, *the Heavens parted*, and the ministering angels beheld the scene. They began to cry." Once again, let us recall that we are discussing *malachim*, spiritual beings with assets and abilities far exceeding those of mere mortals. Why, then, was it necessary for the sky to "open" in order for them to witness the proceedings? Couldn't they just as easily have watched the spectacle from their regular station in the celestial spheres? Did they really need the "Heavens to part" in order to get a better view?

We might be able to arrive at an understanding by examining an issue centered on a Mishnah in Berachos (9:2,5), which states:

עַל בְּשׂוֹרוֹת הַטּוֹבוֹת אוֹמֵר בָּרוּךְ הַטּוֹב וְהַמֵּטִיב, וְעַל שְׁמוּעוֹת רָעוֹת אוֹמֵר בָּרוּךְ דַּיַּן הָאֱמֶת... חַיָּב אָדָם לְבָרֵךְ עַל הָרָעָה כְּשֵׁם שֶׁהוּא מְבָרֵךְ עַל הַטּוֹבָה, שֶׁנֶּאֱמַר וְאָהַבְתָּ אֵת ד' אֱלֹקֶיךָ בְּכָל לְבָבְךָ וּבְכָל נַפְשְׁךָ וּבְכָל מְאֹדֶךָ... בְּכָל מְאֹדֶךָ, בְּכָל מִדָּה וּמִדָּה שֶׁהוּא מוֹדֵד לְךָ הֱוֵי מוֹדֶה לוֹ בִּמְאֹד מְאֹד.

"Upon receiving glad tidings, one recites the blessing of 'Hatov v'hameitiv' (the One Who is good, and bestows goodness). Upon hearing sad news, he recites 'Baruch Dayan Ha'emes' (Blessed is the True Judge)...

> *A person is obligated to bless over misfortune, just as he blesses over fortune. As it states (Devarim 6:5): 'And you shall love Hashem, your G-d, with all of your heart, all of your soul, and all of your **me'od**' (this latter term is usually translated as 'might,' 'wealth,' or 'a lot', but will be expounded upon here based on the sounding of its root-word)... 'All of your **me'od**' (means the following) – through whatever measure (**midd**ah) Hashem metes out (**mod**ed) to you (i.e., whatever happens in one's life), you should give thanks (**mod**eh) to Him with very much (**me'od**) feeling."*

Here and Hereafter

THIS MISHNAH CONTAINS AN INTEGRAL AND profound concept – but the way it is conveyed might almost appear contradictory. The basic theme the Mishnah seeks to impart is a message of *emunah u'bitachon* (faith and trust in Hashem). Whatever Hashem does is for our ultimate benefit. Thus, we bless Him upon learning (for example) that a son was born into the family; and even, G-d forbid, upon suffering a loss, we acknowledge that Hashem is the True Judge of what is ultimately in everyone's best interest. But the Mishnah concludes that we must bless Him for misfortune *just as* we bless over fortune! Why, then, are there two separate blessings? If we truly acknowledge that everything is Divinely calculated for a person's maximum overall welfare, shouldn't we bless "*Hatov v'hameitiv*" in *all* situations – good and "bad"?

We can gain insight from the Gemara in Pesachim (*50a*), which seems to simultaneously concede the point, as well as resolve the issue. The Gemara states that, in essence, this is correct – "*Hatov v'hameitiv*" *should* be recited over everything, good and bad. And so will it be – in the World to Come. In mandating two different blessings, the Mishnah was referring to actual practice here in This World. As mere mortals, our long-range vision here is limited. Thus, we recite "*Hatov v'hameitiv*" over what is *perceptibly* beneficial in the here and now. Regarding tribulation, we suffice with an acknowledgement of faith that deep down we know that Hashem is Merciful and Good and that His acts are precisely and justly calculated. In the World to Come, we will be able to look back on whatever misfortune was suffered and – at that point – recite with a full heart "*Hatov v'hameitiv*" even over (what appeared to be) travails.

R' Shmuel Berenbaum (*cited in Ohel Moshe [R' Moshe Scheinerman], p. 205*) explained the issue of the "parting of the Heavens" in a similar fashion. Of course, the angels could *see* what was happening to Yitzchak from the Heavenly realm without any adjustment for better viewing. But then, of course – from their perch in the celestial heights, where their supernal perception is crystal-clear – they would not shed tears, for they would know without a shadow of a doubt that the event was wholly and completely a happy, beneficial exercise. Thus, in order to elicit crying, it was necessary for Hashem to "part the Heavens," that is, provide them with an "earthly" perception instead of an otherworldly view.

For only in This World is it possible to shed tears. May Hashem help us to merit life in the World to Come, and behold the day when we may look back on everything and pronounce with gratitude and exuberance: "*Hatov v'hameitiv.*"

לזכר ולעילוי נשמות

חיה בת גרשון ע"ה

VAYEITZEI

Share the Wealth

WHAT'S IN A NAME? A LOT. SUCH IS THE CASE with the curious name that Leah bestowed upon her son, Yissachar, in this week's *parshah*. The Torah ties this name to the entity of *s'char* – reward: וַתֹּאמֶר לֵאָה נָתַן אֱלֹקִים שְׂכָרִי... וַתִּקְרָא שְׁמוֹ יִשָּׂשכָר "And Leah said: 'Hashem has granted me my reward...' And she called his name Yissachar" (*Bereishis 30:18*).

Equal Pay

WHAT IS NOTEWORTHY ABOUT THIS ARRANGEMENT IS that the name seems to come with some "excess baggage". Leah was obviously aiming to use the root word שכר; but what is the significance of the two extra letters – יש – that were appended to the beginning?

R' Shlomoh Kluger (*Imrei Shefer*) proffers a fascinating approach to this issue. He bases it on the very last Mishnah in Shas, which discusses the astronomical award reserved for the righteous in the future. The Mishnah states (*Uktzin 3:12*):

Kindly take a moment to study Mishnas Chayim in the merit of
Hinda Varda bas Binyomin a"h
a fellow Jew who passed away with no relatives to arrange Torah study on behalf of her *neshamah*

Vayeitzei / 31

אָמַר רַבִּי יְהוֹשֻׁעַ בֶּן לֵוִי, עָתִיד הַקָּדוֹשׁ בָּרוּךְ הוּא לְהַנְחִיל לְכָל צַדִּיק וְצַדִּיק שְׁלֹשׁ מֵאוֹת וַעֲשָׂרָה עוֹלָמוֹת, שֶׁנֶּאֱמַר לְהַנְחִיל אֹהֲבַי יֵשׁ וְאֹצְרֹתֵיהֶם אֲמַלֵּא.

"R' Yehoshua ben Levi said: In the future, Hakadosh Baruch Hu will bequeath 310 worlds to each and every righteous individual. As it states (Mishlei 8:21): 'To apportion yeish to those who love Me, and I shall fill their treasure-houses.'"

From where does this figure of 310 emerge? On the most basic level, of course, the Mishnah derives it from the *passuk* in Mishlei. The '*yeish*' mentioned here – literally translated as 'something' (i.e., something substantive) – has the numeric equivalent of 310. In stating that the portion of the righteous will be '*yeish*', the *passuk* is conveying that they will receive 310 worlds.

The derivation notwithstanding, the figure is still somewhat mystifying; surely the *passuk* did not merely concoct a random amount. What is the significance of this particular number? Now, it does seem clear where it came from – but still requires some explanation. That is, 310 is half of 620. This is significant, as Rabbinic literature refers often to 620 mitzvos (the 613 Biblical ones, plus the seven Rabbinic enactments [such as the kindling of Chanukah lights and reading Megillas Esther]).

And this is what requires further elucidation. Seemingly, the Mishnah's intent is that the *tzaddikim* receive a "world" for each mitzvah they fulfilled. Thus, having fulfilled all of the mitzvos, they receive... half of the tally? It would seem ludicrous to assume that the *tzaddikim* only performed 50% of the mitzvos; no doubt they did a complete job. If so, however, shouldn't they be receiving a total of 620 worlds?

R' Shlomoh Kluger clarifies what happened to the remaining 310 worlds: they are given to the *tzaddikim*'s wives.

To understand better from where this significant fact is derived, we must turn back to the beginning of time.

Eizer/K'negdo

THE EPISODE OF ADAM'S ACQUISITION OF A MATE can shed much light on this issue. Adam's proffered partner is referred to repeatedly as an *"eizer k'negdo"* – literally, "a helper against him" (*Bereishis* 2:18, 20). Which seems to be a contradiction in terms. If she's a helper, than why and how is she against him?

R' Shlomoh Kluger explains that this very appellation reflects our issue. The reason one's wife receives half of his reward is because of her role as an *eizer*. She assists and encourages her husband's spiritual endeavors in any number of ways. As the Gemara says in Berachos (*17a*): "How do women merit their share?... By facilitating their husbands' Torah-study." As a full partner in his efforts, she gets equal credit; as such, half of the worlds go to him, and the other half to her. In a sense, then, this is the '*k'negdo*' aspect; for by being his *eizer*, she 'takes away' half of his *s'char*!

Yet, in His infinite wisdom, Hashem established this arrangement in such a manner that the husband does not mind at all. Chazal inform us that a person feels envy towards everyone – except his own children. Not only does he not begrudge them their success, but he revels in it. This is because his children are an extension of himself; he is not envious of them, just as he would not be envious of one of his limbs. And so, in contrast to all other creatures, Hashem created man's mate specifically from within his own body. "And Hashem... fashioned the rib that He had taken from man into a woman, and presented her to Adam. And Adam said, 'This... is a bone from my bones, and flesh from my flesh...'" (*Bereishis* 2:22,23). As an entity of his very own self, he is more than happy to share his portion with her.

In any event, a similar arrangement takes place regarding the well-known 'Yissachar-Zevulun' partnership whereby one undertakes the full support of a Torah scholar, enabling the latter to pursue his studies. This partnership, of course, is named for and patterned after the tribes of Yissachar and Zevulun, who had established just such a set-up for themselves; Zevulun engaged in commerce, and used the earnings to allow the Yissacharites to learn.

This, R' Shlomoh Kluger explains, was Leah's intent. Zevulun would be facilitating Yissachar's learning; as such, they would split the *s'char*. Instead of the full amount – all 620 worlds – going to Yissachar, half would go to his brother's *sheivet* (tribe). The name she selected encapsulates this idea. What was he left with? 310 – יש. He receives יש-שכר.

לזכר ולעילוי נשמת

יוסף בן עזרא ע״ה

שרה בת רחמן ע״ה

VAYISHLACH

The Instruction Manual for Galus (Exile)

Knowing the Parshah Can be Good for Your Health...

TO BUILD AND MAINTAIN A THRIVING TORAH enterprise, the efforts of the Ponovezher Rav were intensive and legendary. Thus, he was often forced to visit various far-flung locations across the globe on fundraising excursions. One occasion in New York City found the Ponovezher Rav travelling the subway, carrying around his cache of donations.

Suddenly, he discovered that a group of hoodlums, with malice in their eyes, was closing in around him. Although famed for his intellectual acumen, it didn't take a genius to figure out their designs.

An idea suddenly surfaced in the Ponovezher Rav's mind. In a nonchalant fashion, he slipped out a piece of paper on which was inscribed a certain address (one the Rav knew was close by). Turning to the "gathering crowd", he addressed his would-be attackers with (what appeared to be) all innocence. "Excuse me,"

Kindly take a moment to study Mishnas Chayim in the merit of
Yocheved bas Moshe a"h
A fellow Jew who passed away with no relatives to arrange Torah study on behalf of her *neshamah*

he said, "would any of you happen to know where I must get off to arrive at this address?"

For their part, this development was a boon to the marauders. Much better to attack an elderly man in some dark, quiet alleyway than on a public train in front of a car-full of onlookers. "Well, of course," answered the leader of the pack, with noticeable relish. "That's the next stop. And wouldn't you just know it... We also happen to be getting off at that stop; right, fellahs?"

The car slowed; the bell rang; the doors opened; and they all arose to depart the train. At the last moment, the Ponovezher Rav, turning to his "travelling companions", made a courteous gesture: "After you, gentlemen," he indicated. Out they went; the Rav tarried for a few moments; the doors shut again; and the train continued on, leaving behind a group of frustrated thugs.

When later recounting this episode of deliverance, the Ponovezher Rav was careful to clarify the source of his idea. "Do not think," he explained, "that I came up with this on my own. Rather, I learned it from our forefather, Ya'akov." He went on to relate an event from this week's *parshah*. When Esav and Ya'akov finally met, and the threat of war between them receded, Esav suggested that the two should join together. "And he said, 'Let us journey... and I will travel opposite you'" (*Bereishis 33:12*). What was Ya'akov's response? "Let my master journey ahead, before his servant; I will continue at my slower pace..." (*v. 14*).

It could be that the Ponevezher Rav was actually aided by a whole gamut of Chazal's teachings in this matter. They cautioned to be wary in our dealings with Esav and his descendants, as the danger expressed in the axiom "Esav despises Ya'akov" is ever-present. Thus, for example, the Mishnah states in Avodah Zarah (*2:1*):

לֹא יִתְיַחֵד אָדָם עִמָּהֶן, מִפְּנֵי שֶׁחֲשׁוּדִין עַל שְׁפִיכוּת דָּמִים.

"A Jew should avoid seclusion with an idolator, for he is suspected of homicidal tendencies."

Elaborating on this theme, the Gemara (*Avodah Zarah 25b*) addresses a situation reminiscent of that of the Ponevezher Rav: "If they ask him where he is headed, he should respond by widening the distance between them." As proof, the Gemara proceeds to cite none other than the verse mentioned above, whereby Ya'akov implores Esav to continue on without him (*cf. Peninim Mishulchan Gavohah, parshas Vayishlach*).

The Magic Words

IN ACTUALITY, FROM TIME IMMEMORIAL KLAL Yisrael has consulted our *parshah* for guidance in navigating the perils of *galus*. The Ramban states explicitly that Ya'akov's dealings with Esav will duplicate themselves throughout the generations, as *b'nei* Yisrael live under the dominion of the children of Esav. Thus we find, for example, that the Midrash records how R' Yannai – upon his periodic visits to the Roman capital on a communal endeavor – would first peer into *parshas* Vayishlach for guidance (*Bereishis Rabbah 78:18*).

Perhaps one of the best known examples of a generational leader who utilized the lessons of this *parshah* to aid his brethren was the venerated R' Chaim Volozhiner. Many times his intervention was necessary to prevent the implementation of yet another of the many harsh decrees being promulgated in Russia at that time. Of course, he engaged in heartfelt prayer, emulating this measure used by Ya'akov when he anticipated the meeting with Esav.

And then there was the other aspect of Ya'akov's preparatory measures.

One time, R' Chaim journeyed to the halls of power in St. Petersberg, in the hopes of beseeching the notorious prime-minister of Czar Alexander I. The Jew-hatred of this particular official was so intense, that he had declared he would not speak to or even look at a Jew. Nevertheless, as he was the driving force behind the latest anti-Semitic decree aimed at stifling Jewish education, R' Chaim was determined to secure a meeting.

To entice the minister, R' Chaim sent a message upon his arrival in the capital city. He made it known that he wished to see the official, and tell him only two words. To "sweeten the deal", R'

Chaim added that should he go over the count by even a single word, the prime minister would be authorized to kill him.

This caught the minister's attention. He summoned the Jewish sage before him – no doubt eager for R' Chaim to falter in his challenge. Appearing before the official, R' Chaim laid down a bag stuffed with silver coins on the table, and proceeded to relate two Russian words: "*Byeri I'molchi*" – Take, and be quiet.

The decree never came to fruition. R' Chaim had duplicated the strategy employed by Ya'akov, who sent Esav an elaborate gift in order to appease his anger (*Avi Hayeshivos*).

לזכר ולעילוי נשמת
רבקה רחל ע"ה בת ר' ישראל צבי נ"י

VAYEISHEV

Origin of the Blood Libel

THIS WEEK'S *PARSHAH* RELATES THE EPISODE OF THE struggle between Yosef and his brothers, leading to *mechiras* Yosef (the selling of Yosef into slavery) at his brothers' hands. To prevent their father Ya'akov from identifying them as the party responsible for the disappearance of his most beloved son, they arranged for matters to appear differently: "And they took Yosef's *kesones* (tunic)... and they dipped the tunic in (goat's) blood... They brought it to their father... and they said, '... Is this your son's tunic?' He recognized it, and said, 'This is my son's tunic; a vicious beast has devoured him. Yosef has been torn asunder!'" (*Bereishis 37:32,33*).

As is well known, the ramifications of this act were astounding. With Yosef en route to Mitzrayim, the whole chain of events leading to the eventual Exodus from Egypt and the emergence of Klal Yisrael as a Torah nation was set in motion. But the deed also carried some grievous consequences, effects which – as we shall see – linger to this very day.

KINDLY TAKE A MOMENT TO STUDY MISHNAS CHAYIM IN THE MERIT OF
FRAYDA BAS HARRY A"H
A FELLOW JEW WHO PASSED AWAY WITH NO RELATIVES TO ARRANGE TORAH STUDY ON BEHALF OF HER NESHAMAH

Atonement – in Installments

MANY ARE FAMILIAR WITH RASHI'S COMMENTS (*Shemos 32:34*) about the enduring effects of the *Cheit Ha'eigel* (Sin of the Golden Calf). Whenever punishment is visited upon Yisrael, a measure of severity is added to achieve yet another degree of atonement for this national sin. Somewhat less known is the fact that this is not the only sin on whose account the Jewish people still suffer.

This is apparent from the Yom Kippur Temple service. An important detail about the garments worn by the officiating Kohen Gadol (High Priest) is recorded in the Mishnah (*Yoma 3:7*):

בַּשַּׁחַר הָיָה לוֹבֵשׁ שֶׁל שְׁמוֹנָה עָשָׂר מָנֶה, וּבֵין הָעַרְבַּיִם שֶׁל שְׁנֵים עָשָׂר מָנֶה.

> "In the morning, he wore garments worth eighteen maneh; in the afternoon, of twelve maneh."

The reason the garments worn for the morning service were of superior quality (and hence more expensive) than the set used in the afternoon is because it was in the morning that the chief atonement rituals took place (*Rashi, Yoma 35b*). To be sure, it was actually one specific garment that was "upgraded" for the morning service: the Rambam (*Hilchos Klei Hamikdash, 8:3*) identifies it as none other than the *kesones* (priestly tunic).

Why such emphasis on this particular garment, that it should figure so prominently in the atonement ceremony? The *Meshech Chachmah* (*Acharei Mos*) states that the use of the priestly tunic at this time serves to atone for that long-ago sin, also involving a tunic – that is, the selling of Yosef (who was stripped by his brothers of his *kesones*). He cites the Gemara in Zevachim (*86b*), which states that the *kesones* secures special atonement for the sin of *shefichas damim* (murder – literally, 'spilling of blood'). As proof, the Gemara quotes the *passuk* from our *parshah*: "And they dipped (Yosef's) *kesones* in the blood." A *kesones* atoning for a *kesones*.

Thus we see that every year, a significant component of the Yom Kippur service was conducted specifically to atone for the sin of *mechiras* Yosef. Apparently, this was a very necessary step, for – in a fashion reminiscent of the *Cheit Ha'eigel* – the specter of this sin, as well, hangs over Klal Yisrael in every generation (*cf. Midrash Mishlei, §1*).

R' Elchanan Wasserman, HY"D, (*Kovetz Ma'amarim*) **Dangerous Irony**

R' Elchanan Wasserman, HY"D, (*Kovetz Ma'amarim*) goes one step further in revealing the enduring consequences of this deed. He focused on the bizarre phenomenon known as the "blood libel," which all too often would raise its ugly head. The gentiles would claim that Jews had abducted and killed a non-Jewish child to use his blood in the baking of matzos (an accusation that was once again raised by some Palestinian official approximately a month prior to this writing). Over the course of Jewish history, this claim was raised – with often tragic results. Much Jewish blood was spilled in retaliation for this alleged crime.

From where did this surface? Such nonsensical accusations, which nonetheless led to great persecution! R' Elchanan posited that this was Divinely orchestrated, an act of Divine retribution for the sin of *mechiras* Yosef.

What seems difficult to understand is how this conforms to the notion of *middah keneged middah* (measure for measure). In what way does the punishment relate to the crime? On the surface, of course, the two revolve around the spilling of blood ("And they dipped the *kesones* in blood..."). Perhaps, however, the connection can be understood on a somewhat deeper level.

R' Moshe Shternbuch (*Ta'am V'da'as*) raises an interesting point: The brothers kept the true fate of Yosef from their father. But why did they attribute his disappearance to a wild animal? Why not report a much more common (and hence more plausible) cause, such as attack from bandits?

R' Shternbuch explains that they actually sought to spare their father further pain. Ya'akov had sent his son on a mission (to check on his brothers) from which he never returned. According to the *halachah* (*Magen Avraham §603*), the sender in such a scenario bears a measure of culpability, and must therefore seek atonement. But this holds true only if the messenger died of a somewhat common cause; had his death come about through unusual means, no atonement is necessary. That is why the brothers did not select a more common cause; this way Ya'akov would not hold himself responsible and undertake a rigorous and painful process of penitence.

While well-intentioned, the irony is glaring. They didn't want their father to suffer; they even risked getting caught to spare him trouble. So why did they kidnap his most beloved son?

Perhaps this might account for the *middah keneged middah* aspect of the blood libel, for the form of the punishment is just as ironic. Among the narratives of the horrors of the Holocaust, we find that the Nazis, *yimach shemam,* would sometimes couch their terror in "humanitarian" terms. On some occasions, they would select the town *shochet* (butcher) as the first target of their persecutions. They would claim that his method of dispatching chickens was cruel and barbaric. Standing up for the chickens' welfare, they proceeded to murder the man in cold blood.

The blood libel also shared this ironic element. Those who raised the prospect were obviously so concerned for the supposed victims. So they responded with an outpouring of violence against untold innocent Jewish men, women, and children – may Hashem avenge their blood.

לזכר ולעילוי נשמות
משולם זושא בן יצחק אייזיק ע"ה
חנה גיטל בת צבי ע"ה

MIKEITZ

The Royalty of the Chashmona'im

WOULD YOU LIKE TO BE PRESIDENT OF THE UNITED States? This has been the enduring dream of countless millions of people. Putting aside the fact that a good percentage of actual White House residents were only too happy to leave at their term's end, the attainment of this high office is considered the crowning achievement of a lifetime. The glory and prestige that go with it make this position perhaps the most coveted in the world.

OF COURSE, THERE WAS A TIME WHEN THE PREVALENT leadership role in most countries was that of absolute monarch. *King for a Day...* Imagine the grandeur experienced by actually being a king! The wealth, splendor and power of these sovereigns was legendary.

At least, this is how most of the world views it. One would have thought that the great men of Yisrael, with their elevated perspectives, would not harbor aspirations of such pomp and glory.

Kindly take a moment to study Mishnas Chayim in the merit of
Moshe Aharon *ben* Gedalyah *a"h*
a fellow Jew who passed away with no relatives to arrange Torah study on behalf of his *neshamah*

And yet, it appears that this was indeed the case. Take David and Shlomoh, for instance: men of unparalleled spirituality and Torah wisdom. At the same time, they greatly valued *malchus* (kingship) and sought to acquire and retain royal power. How could such pristine, sacred souls be so desirous of the epitome of earthy glory and material wealth and power?

We can gain some insight by focusing on the Chashmona'im (Hasmoneans), the family that figured so prominently in the Chanukah story.

THE EVENTS ASSOCIATED WITH THE CHANUKAH story are recorded in the Gemara in Shabbos (*21b*):

Beginning of the Dynasty
"When the Greeks entered into the Temple, they defiled all the oil within the Sanctuary. When Malchus Beis Chashmona'i (the regime of the House of the Chashmona'im) became ascendant and prevailed over the enemy, they then conducted a search (in the Temple) but could only find one flask of oil... which had only enough lighting power to kindle the Menorah for a single day. A miracle was wrought through it, and they were able to light with this oil for eight days..."

As well-known as this narrative is, it does contain a somewhat surprising statement concerning the chronology of events. Chazal are always quite particular in their wording. Notice how they refer to this small band of fighters who took on the formidable enemy: "When Malchus Beis Chashmona'i... prevailed over the enemy..." They are being called "Malchus Beis Chashmona'i" even as they were still engaged in the struggle! Our usual understanding is response to the persecutions of the Greek regime, the family of Chashmona'im waged a lopsided war, which they miraculously won. In the aftermath of their improbable victory and the miracle of the Menorah, they established their own reign, as dominion once again returned to Yisrael. From the Gemara's description, however, it seems that they were already considered "Malchus Beis Chashmsona'i," and *then* they vanquished the enemy!

Based on the teachings of the Alter from Kelm, R' Yeruchem Olshin (*Yerach L'mo'adim, ma'amar 33*) elucidates the issue by examining the Torah's perspective of "*malchus.*"

Sharing and Bearing the Burden

OF COURSE, THE ALTER EXPLAINS, THE RIGHTEOUS David and Shlomoh were not interested in the ephemeral trappings of riches and glory. Their desire for *malchus* stemmed not from base ambition, but from a truly altruistic yearning for a much more substantial entity. That is, they sought to perform *chessed* (kindness) for their fellow Jews. The power and status of kingship would enable them to reach the maximum number of people, helping them in the most optimal way possible. Indeed, they excelled in the *middah* (attribute) of "*nosei b'ol im chaveiro*" – bearing the burden of one's neighbor with him. The Alter terms this particular *middah* as the "*k'lil hama'alos*" – the supreme value. Dovid and Shlomoh empathized with the needs of the entire Jewish community and sought to alleviate their travails.

The Mishnah in Sanhedrin (*2:8*) relates some laws that pertain to the king:

אֵין רוֹכְבִין עַל סוּסוֹ, וְאֵין יוֹשְׁבִין עַל כִּסְאוֹ, וְאֵין מִשְׁתַּמְּשִׁין בְּשַׁרְבִיטוֹ, וְאֵין רוֹאִין אוֹתוֹ כְּשֶׁהוּא מִסְתַּפֵּר.

"One may not ride on (the king's) horse, nor sit on his throne, nor use his scepter, nor view him as his hair is being cut."

These are some examples of the honor that we must accord the king. While it might almost seem obvious, the question can be raised: Why, in fact, must we honor a king? Is it because of his power? His vast wealth? The Alter from Kelm asserts that the honor due a king stems from the very trait discussed above. It is because he possesses and exercises this most admirable of all traits – being *nosei b'ol im chaveiro* that he deserves such respectful treatment.

This, explains R' Yeruchem, is the intent behind the Gemara's characterization of "Malchus Beis Chashmona'i." Of course, their actual reign began only after the enemy was vanquished and deposed. When the Gemara states that it was Malchus Beis Chashmona'i that waged the war and defeated the Greeks, it is not referring to the established regime. Rather, the Gemara is referring to the *attribute* of *malchus*, the quality that the Chashmona'im assumed in their efforts to deliver their brethren.

In other words, the Gemara's intent is that in undertaking the campaign, the Chashmona'im were *behaving* like royalty. As we have learned, the quintessential monarch, in the Torah's perspective, is one whose focus is not on his palatial estates or his vast treasures; he does not view his crown as a personal achievement, the realization of a dream of the ultimate grandeur. Rather, he effectively annuls his own self, devoting his strength and resources to helping his people. And this was the approach that the Chashmona'im adopted, putting themselves at great risk for the sole purpose of being *nosei b'ol* with the nation, seeking their safety and deliverance. They utilized the quality of "*malchus*" in order to fight against the enemy. Hashem smiled upon their efforts, delivering through them a miraculous victory on behalf of His people.

לזכר ולעילוי נשמות
נתנאל בן משה ע"ה
שינדיל דבורה בת דוד ע"ה

VAYIGASH

On That Day

THEY SAY THAT BIG THINGS COME IN SMALL packages. This week's *parshah* conveys an invaluable lesson, with astounding ramifications. And it is all contained within two simple words.

Case Closed

THE *PARSHAH* OPENS WITH THE BROTHERS returning before Yosef with Yehudah as their spokesman. Up until this point, the *Shevatim* (Tribes) had been beset by an almost unrelenting series of perplexing and devastating blows, beginning from the start of their first foray to Mitzrayim. When originally appearing before the "Egyptian" viceroy to purchase food, they were suddenly and strangely singled out for harsh treatment. Accusations of spying were hurled against them, and they were forced to go to extraordinary lengths – to return with their youngest brother, Binyamin – in order to establish their innocence. All the while, their brother Shimon was incarcerated as a hostage.

KINDLY TAKE A MOMENT TO STUDY MISHNAS CHAYIM IN THE MERIT OF
BAILA BAS AHARON A"H
A FELLOW JEW WHO PASSED AWAY WITH NO RELATIVES TO ARRANGE TORAH STUDY ON BEHALF OF HER *NESHAMAH*

Their anxiety mounted on their journey homeward when they found, to their shock, that the money with which they had purchased their goods had somehow made its way back into their sacks. The *passuk* describes their state of mind upon making this discovery: "And their hearts left them; terrified, they exclaimed to each other, 'What is this that Hashem has done to us?'" (*Bereishis 42:28*).

Further surprises were in store. Upon returning to Mitzrayim, they attempted to pre-empt further tragedy by telling the viceroy's attendant about the strange incident with their money. "Nothing to worry about," they were told. "It must be that your G-d granted you a windfall." They were invited to dine at the viceroy's house; upon taking their places, they noticed that the seating arrangements conformed exactly to their respective ages. "And they sat before him – the eldest according to his age, and the youngest according to his age; and the men were greatly confounded" (*ibid. 43:33*). Strange; nevertheless, everything seemed to be going much smoother. Shimon was back with them, the viceroy seemed to be pleased, and soon they were on their way back home. It appeared that their whole ordeal was finally over, and they could return their father's beloved, youngest son back to him, safe and sound.

In another moment, the tables turned dramatically, once again. They were hauled back before the viceroy; his silver goblet was missing, only to be found... in the sack of Binyamin! It seemed that the worst had come to pass: were they to return to their father without Binyamin? He would never survive the tragedy. So here they were: the climax of this long string of bewildering and wrenching events found them begging to remain as perpetual slaves to the viceroy so that Binyamin, at least, could return.

And then the seminal revelation burst forth. With two simple words, everything became crystal clear. The mysterious events, the bizarre treatment, all their questions – in a single instant, it all dissipated. The man said to them: "**Ani Yosef** – I am Yosef" (*ibid. 45:3*).

And So It Will Be...

DRAMATIC AS THIS EPIC NARRATIVE IS, THE implications reverberate well beyond the brothers' own situation. In fact, as expounded in the *Sefer Ohel Moshe* (*Badei Nechamah, ch. 7*), this event foreshadows the nature of Hashem's future revelation upon Yisrael and the world.

As a person goes through life, he inevitably encounters challenges and travails. This he observes about his own life, as well as that of others. He might come across suffering and misery, and the meaning of it all escapes him.

Indeed, this is the nature of This World – especially in a time such as ours, when the *hester panim* (concealment of the Divine Presence) is so substantial. The truth is that there are many things that are simply beyond our ability to comprehend for the time being – so long as the righteous but secret calculations remain hidden from us. As the Mishnah states (*Avos 4:15*):

אֵין בְּיָדֵינוּ לֹא מִשַּׁלְוַת הָרְשָׁעִים וְאַף לֹא מִיִּסּוּרֵי הַצַּדִּיקִים.

"We are not privy (in This World) to the reasons for which some wicked people experience tranquility, while there are righteous who suffer affliction."

But the test and the challenge for us is not to allow these perplexities to overwhelm us, but to remain steadfast in our faith that "The Rock, His acts are perfect, and all of His ways are just" (*Devarim 32:4*). Everything that occurs is orchestrated by Hashem for maximum benefit. And the day will yet come when these calculations will be revealed, and all creatures of the earth will recognize and give thanks for what was ultimately a blessing. The lesson of *"Ani Yosef"* demonstrates to us how a lifetime or thousands of years of suffering and confusion will take on an entirely new light in the blink of an eye.

In this regard, the *Ohel Moshe* (citing the *Me'am Lo'ez*) relates a remarkable story concerning the Ramban. A disciple of his had fallen deathly ill, and the sage went to visit him. As an extremely pious and spiritual personage – and a Kabbalistic master – the

Ramban perceived in the unfolding events a Divinely orchestrated opportunity. He approached his disciple with a singular request.

Handing him an amulet with Kabbalistic inscriptions, the Ramban issued to his disciple some crucial instructions. "As you journey to the Next World, take this amulet with you; it will allow you to pass through numerous Heavenly gates, until you arrive at a most elevated celestial chamber. Once there, I bid you to ask the following questions I have that concern the welfare of Klal Yisrael." With that, the Ramban handed him a piece of paper on which were listed the vital queries. He asked his disciple to return to him in a dream to relate the answers.

Some time after the disciple passed away, sure enough, the Ramban received a visitation. "It is as you had said," the disciple reported. "The sacred implement you gave me opened all doors, allowing me to ascend to the chamber of which you spoke." The Ramban, obviously, was anxious to hear the answers he so desperately sought. The reply, however, came as follows: "But *Rebbi*, when I came to present the questions, I suddenly realized – from that standpoint in the World of Ultimate Truth – that the questions, in fact, were not questions at all!"

לזכר ולעילוי נשמת

ברײנא בת נתן ע״ה

VAYECHI

The Fate of the Ten Lost Tribes of Yisrael

THIS WEEK'S *PARSHAH* CONTAINS THE SECTION IN which Ya'akov bestows a unique blessing on each of his children, who comprise the future tribes of Yisrael. A curious *passuk* appears at the completion of this section: כָּל־אֵלֶּה שִׁבְטֵי יִשְׂרָאֵל שְׁנֵים עָשָׂר וְזֹאת אֲשֶׁר־דִּבֶּר לָהֶם אֲבִיהֶם וַיְבָרֶךְ אוֹתָם "All of these are the twelve tribes of Yisrael, and this is what their father spoke to them and blessed them" (*Bereishis 49:28*). While it might seem straightforward enough, these words actually almost demand explanation; they seem completely unnecessary. Here we are, almost at the end of Sefer Bereishis, nearing the completion of the *parshah* and having just gone through a somewhat detailed account of Ya'akov's final, individualized charge to each of his children. If at this point you need to be reminded that the tribes of Yisrael are twelve in number and that what you just read were, in fact, *berachos* – well, something at least *seems* to be wrong.

Kindly take a moment to study Mishnas Chayim in the merit of
Lilly bas Gershon A"H
a fellow Jew who passed away with no relatives to arrange Torah study on behalf of her *neshamah*

R' Yechezkel Abramsky demonstrates that, in fact, a vital message is contained herein. The *passuk* is expressing no less than a guarantee of the eternal existence of the entirety of Klal Yisrael, that never shall even a single tribe disappear. Ya'akov gave his children an additional, special blessing, assuring them to this effect. This is the meaning of the *passuk*. The content of what their father spoke and blessed them with was exactly this: that forever, the tribes of Yisrael shall be twelve in number (*Sefer Hazikaron*, p. 177).

The Lost Tribes: How "Lost" are They?

WHILE THE MESSAGE IS POWERFUL, THE QUESTION arises as to how this complies with (at least one opinion) of the following Mishnah, which discusses the fate of the tribes. As is well known, ten tribes were eventually exiled by the king of Assyria, leaving only Yehudah and Binyamin behind. The Mishnah in Sanhedrin (*10:3*) deals with whether or not these "lost" tribes are ever to return:

עֲשֶׂרֶת הַשְּׁבָטִים אֵינָן עֲתִידִין לַחֲזוֹר, שֶׁנֶּאֱמַר: וַיַּשְׁלִכֵם אֶל אֶרֶץ אַחֶרֶת כַּיּוֹם הַזֶּה, מָה הַיּוֹם הַזֶּה הוֹלֵךְ וְאֵינוֹ חוֹזֵר, אַף הֵם הוֹלְכִים וְאֵינָם חוֹזְרִים, דִּבְרֵי רַבִּי עֲקִיבָא. רַבִּי אֱלִיעֶזֶר אוֹמֵר, כַּיּוֹם הַזֶּה, מָה הַיּוֹם מַאֲפִיל וּמֵאִיר, אַף עֲשֶׂרֶת הַשְּׁבָטִים שֶׁאָפַל לָהֶן, כָּךְ עָתִיד לְהָאִיר לָהֶן.

"The ten tribes are not destined to ever return. As it states (Devarim 29:27): 'And He sent them to a different land as of this day' (the Mishnah will understand this phrase as describing the nature of their exile): Just as a day passes, never to return, so, too, the exiles have gone away, never to return. This is the opinion of R' Akiva. R' Eliezer (offers an alternative explanation of this phrase): Just as a day begins with darkness but turns to light, the situation of the ten tribes began with darkness but will end with light (i.e., they will return)."

According to R' Akiva, at least, the sad fact is that the ten tribes are lost forever. But... what about the promise?

The Gemara in Megillah (*14b*) issues a remarkable statement: יִרְמְיָה... הָלַךְ לְהַחֲזִיר עֲשֶׂרֶת הַשְּׁבָטִים... וְיֹאשִׁיָּהוּ בֶּן אָמוֹן מָלַךְ עֲלֵיהֶן. "The Prophet Yirmiyahu went to bring back the ten tribes (to Eretz Yisrael)... (he did so) and they were ruled over by King Yoshiyahu ben Amon."

While this appears to be a "bright spot" for the *Aseres Hashevatim*, it also, at first glance, seems to complicate matters. How does this statement concur with the opinion of R' Akiva, who held that these tribes were never to return! Rashi (*Sanhedrin 110b*) supplies the answer, explaining that, in truth, Yirmiyahu only returned a small percentage of the ten tribes. The vast majority stayed in exile, where – according to R' Akiva – they will forever remain.

It appears, however, that we are still left with the issue of Ya'akov's promise and blessing that no *sheivet* would ever be forgotten. Was this blessing fulfilled through the return of a mere tiny percentage of the *Aseres Hashevatim*?

It should be noted that the Maharal states unequivocally: "*Chas v'Shalom!* One cannot think that a single *sheivet* will be lost from Yisrael!" (*Netzach Yisrael, ch. 34*). More insight on the matter can be deduced from Rashi himself (*ibid.*). From his comments, it appears that the entire dispute between R' Akiva and R' Eliezer was actually quite limited in scope. That is, the entire discussion revolves around just that first generation – the ones who were actually exiled, for they themselves were thoroughly wicked. Their descendants, however, don't share the same blame and are thus eligible to return – even in the opinion of R' Akiva.

The Happy Ending

AS SUCH, IT APPEARS THAT THE BEAUTIFUL description in the following Midrashic statement would concur with both views. The Mishnah in Avos (5:5) lists ten special items that were created during twilight, immediately preceding the very first Shabbos at the time of Creation. One of these is the ram that was eventually sacrificed by Avraham after the trial of *Akeidas Yitzchak* (Binding of Yitzchak). The Medrash (*Pirkei D'R'Eliezer, ch.*

31) recounts how every part of this ram was put to use, including its horns, which were fashioned into shofars:

"The left horn was blown by Hashem at Har Sinai. The right one is greater than the left. It will be blown in the future to herald the return of the ten tribes. As it states (*Yeshayah 27:13*): וְהָיָה בַּיּוֹם הַהוּא יִתָּקַע בְּשׁוֹפָר גָּדוֹל וּבָאוּ הָאֹבְדִים בְּאֶרֶץ אַשּׁוּר וְהַנִּדָּחִים בְּאֶרֶץ מִצְרָיִם וְהִשְׁתַּחֲווּ לַד' בְּהַר הַקֹּדֶשׁ בִּירוּשָׁלָיִם 'And it will be on that day, a great shofar will be blown, and those lost in the land of Assyria will come, as well as the dispersed in the land of Egypt; and they shall bow to Hashem on the holy mountain, in Yerushalayim.'"

May we merit to hear this shofar, speedily in our days!

לזכר ולעילוי נשמת
ישראל צבי בן חיים יהושע פאלק ע"ה

SEFER SHEMOS
ספר שמות

לזכר ולעילוי נשמות
בערל בן הערש ע"ה
מלכה בת יוחנן ע"ה

SHEMOS

Out-Scheming the Schemer

Admirable Courage – or Reckless Endangerment?

THE HEROIC EXPLOITS OF THE HEBREW MIDWIVES Shifrah and Pu'ah are related in this week's *parshah*. In connection with his diabolical plan to thwart the proliferation of Jewish male babies, Pharaoh instructs the midwives: "When you see on the birthing stool that it is a boy, you shall kill him" (*Shemos 1:16*). They, however, withstood the pressure: "The midwives feared Hashem and did not do as Pharaoh instructed... (instead) they 'gave life' to the male children" (*ibid. v. 17*). Chazal comment that their defiance of Pharaoh, as reflected in this verse, was actually twofold; not only did they desist from harming the babies, but they actually 'gave life' to them – that is, they nurtured them with food and drink (*Sotah 11b*).

There appears to be a perplexing element to this last aspect; while clearly brave and audacious, the question arises: was the risk really worth it?

Kindly take a moment to study Mishnas Chayim in the merit of
Berel ben Max *a"h*
a fellow Jew who passed away with no relatives to arrange Torah study on behalf of his *neshamah*

Consider the Mishnah's comment regarding an event connected with the *halachos* of reciting *Keriyas Shema*. Beis Shamai and Beis Hillel disputed the intent of the Torah's directive that the Shema is to be recited בְּשָׁכְבְּךָ וּבְקוּמֶךָ – "When you lie down and when you arise" (*Devarim 6:7*). Beis Shamai understood this phrase in the literal sense; hence, they held that one recites the Shema in a horizontal position at night, while in the morning, one recites the prayer while standing. Beis Hillel, on the other hand, interpreted the verse as a mere reference to the time of recital, i.e., the time of day when people generally lie down (night) and when they typically arise (morning). Regarding the position of the reader, however, they felt that the Torah was not particular; a person could stand, sit, or walk during either the daytime or nighttime recital. The Mishnah (*Berachos 1:3*) records the practice of one sage who adopted Beis Shamai's stringency:

אָמַר רַבִּי טַרְפוֹן, אֲנִי הָיִיתִי בָא בַדֶּרֶךְ, וְהִטֵּתִי לִקְרוֹת כְּדִבְרֵי בֵית שַׁמַּאי, וְסִכַּנְתִּי בְעַצְמִי מִפְּנֵי הַלִּסְטִים. אָמְרוּ לוֹ, כְּדַי הָיִיתָ לָחוּב בְּעַצְמְךָ, שֶׁעָבַרְתָּ עַל דִּבְרֵי בֵית הִלֵּל.

"R' Tarfon said: 'I was once travelling on the way (at night), and I stopped to recite the Shema while reclining, in accordance with the opinion of Beis Shamai; I had even placed myself in danger to do so, due to the threat of bandits.' They said to him: 'You were actually worthy of death due to your actions, for having disregarded the opinion of Beis Hillel.'"

So steadfast had R' Tarfon been in his adherence to this directive that he followed the stringency of Beis Shamai (of pausing and "laying" for the nighttime Shema), even to the point of risking an attack by marauders. Far from crediting his gallantry, however, his disputants accused him of reckless behavior. He could have avoided danger by following Beis Hillel and reciting the Shema while continuing on his journey. Leaving himself open to harm, they felt, was actually a grievous act of near suicide.

In a similar vein, R' Yosef Shaul Halevi Natanzon (*Divrei Shaul, parshas Shemos*) wondered about the midwives' actions. True, they were confronted with a command to commit murder – one of the three cardinal sins for which a Jew must be willing to sacrifice his life to avoid the violation. But wouldn't it have sufficed to merely refrain from killing the children? Why did they have to add fuel to the fire by going so far as to supply the children with extra care and nourishment? This flagrant defiance of Pharaoh's will would certainly raise his ire and unnecessarily increase the danger to themselves! How were they authorized to go so far?

In a brilliant exposition, R' Yosef Shaul demonstrates that these women were not some foolhardy martyrs but actually quite clever and resourceful strategists.

Pharaoh's PR Problem

It seems that – at this point in the narrative, at least – Pharaoh was still concerned with appearances and sought to conduct his baby-killings in a clandestine manner. As such, he much preferred that the murders be perpetrated on as-of-yet unborn children, which could presumably be dispatched without raising too much of an alarm. (Once the babies emerged alive, there was no longer a possibility of a "stillborn" alibi.)

The midwives were fully aware of Pharaoh's concern – and they took full advantage of it. They concocted a scheme whereby they could simultaneously assist the Jewish mothers and neutralize any potential complaint against themselves.

Essentially, this is what they told Pharaoh:

"We would like to cooperate with your infanticide plot, but there's one problem. As employees of the Egyptian establishment, the Jewish mothers will be wary of us; as such, they may very well attempt to give birth on their own, without calling for our help. By the time we are on hand, the babies will already be born, and it will be too late for any covert assassinations.

Shemos / 59

"But we have a plan," they continued, "to win the confidence of the Jewish women. If we provide care and succor to the newborns – in apparent contradiction of your anti-Hebrew campaign – the mothers will feel more secure with us. The word will get around that we midwives are to be trusted after all, and so the mothers will begin to summon us even before they give birth."

This, explains the Divrei Shaul, was the midwives' clever ruse. By actively lending a helping hand to the mothers and their newborns, they were not recklessly risking Pharaoh's wrath. On the contrary, they put him in a nice little bind while protecting their own skins. To Pharaoh they could claim that their efforts were necessary to lull the mothers into complacency, so his instructions would eventually be carried out. But their true aim was the nurturing itself. They figured out a way to keep the babies alive – happy and healthy – right under Pharaoh's nose.

לזכר ולעילוי נשמת
פיגא בת דוב ע"ה

VA'EIRA

Honored Pharaoh

LET US IMAGINE FOR A MOMENT THAT WE WERE granted an opportunity to enter the Egyptian royal court some time during the Exodus saga.

We are in the midst of an imposing edifice, an exquisite and stately hall. An array of uniformed guards and important-looking personages fills the premises. Pharaoh himself, of course, occupies center stage in this regal scene. Resplendent in his royal garments, he sits elevated on his gilded throne, flanked all around by advisors and nobility. All eyes are turned toward him, and not a sound is to be heard from the entire audience as they await a signal from their monarch.

Suddenly, the solemn aura is interrupted; a curious noise emanates from the monarch – from his abdomen, specifically.

"Gribbit."

The call is subsequently answered by another, this one coming from one of the officials. "Gribbit! Gribbit!" In moments, the whole room is croaking, moaning and groaning. With hands on

---

Kindly take a moment to study Mishnas Chayim in the merit of
Howard ben Isadore *a"h*
a fellow Jew who passed away with no relatives to arrange Torah study on behalf of his *neshamah*

their stomachs in a futile attempt to squash the noise and quell the pain caused by the amphibious invaders lodged in their intestines, the Mitzrim (Egyptians) squirm in agony as the hall erupts into a symphony of resounding ribbits.

Laughingstock

THE SCENARIO PORTRAYED ABOVE IS LAID OUT BY R' Leib Chasman (presented here with some minor stylistic variations) in his *sefer Ohr Yaheil* (vol. II); he describes the substantial denigration that was visited upon the Mitzrim as part of their overall retribution package.

This element seems to have been a significant factor in the Mitzrim's ordeal. When Hashem deemed that the time of the wicked ones' downfall had arrived, it was total. Not only were they presented with harsh punishment, but with shame and disgrace as well. And this aspect was to be noted and highlighted by the Jewish people. As the verse states:

וּלְמַעַן תְּסַפֵּר בְּאָזְנֵי בִנְךָ וּבֶן־בִּנְךָ אֵת אֲשֶׁר **הִתְעַלַּלְתִּי** בְּמִצְרַיִם וְאֶת־אֹתֹתַי אֲשֶׁר־שַׂמְתִּי בָם.

"In order that you relate in the ears of your son and your grandchild that which I made mockery of Mitzrayim and the signs which I set among them" (Shemos 10:2).

The Ramban (*ibid.*) goes even further in describing the pathetic state to which Pharaoh was reduced. After so many warnings and so many abuses, an element of Pharaoh's free will was diminished by Hashem; yet, he still suffered the consequences of his (now uncontrollable) obstinacy. Thus, Hashem hardened his heart, and he continued to refuse to free the Jews; and then he was battered for retaining them as his subjects. In effect, Pharaoh – as a result of his long and evil record – had now become Hashem's plaything. The Ramban ascribes the following verse to Pharaoh's situation: "The One Who dwells in the Heavens will laugh; Hashem will heap scorn upon him" (*Tehillim* 2:4).

Reb Mordechai Pesach Poderevsky of Kobrin merited to attend to the Chafetz Chaim toward the end of the sage's life. Late one Friday night, at around midnight, Reb Mordechai was walking past the Chafetz Chaim's house, when the sweet sound of Torah learning grabbed his attention. The temptation to view the tzaddik "in action" was too great, and so the attendant drew close to the window and peered inside.

He saw the Chafetz Chaim reviewing the weekly parshah (which happened to be this week's parshah – Va'eira). Immersed in the material, the Chafetz Chaim would emit a note of astonishment as he went through each of the makkos: "Ai! Ai!" At one point, Reb Mordechai witnessed a reaction no one had ever seen before: in the middle of the plague of boils (when the magicians were so stricken they could not even come to court), the Chafetz Chaim was literally laughing out loud! (Sichos HaChafetz Chaim)

With All Due Respect

YET, IN THE MIDST OF THIS MONUMENTAL enterprise of humiliating retribution, Moshe and Aharon are given a directive from Hashem that is most unexpected in its nature. The verse in this week's *parshah* states:

וַיְדַבֵּר ה' אֶל־מֹשֶׁה וְאֶל־אַהֲרֹן וַיְצַוֵּם אֶל־בְּנֵי יִשְׂרָאֵל וְאֶל־פַּרְעֹה מֶלֶךְ מִצְרָיִם...

"And Hashem spoke to Moshe and Aharon, and He commanded them concerning B'nei Yisrael and concerning Pharaoh, king of Egypt" (Shemos 6:13).

What was the nature of this "commandment... concerning Pharaoh"? What exactly were Moshe and Aharon supposed to do? Rashi clarifies the details: "Hashem instructed them that their conversations with Pharaoh should be carried out respectfully." In other words, at the same time that Pharaoh and his countrymen were being subjected to degradation of astronomical proportions, Moshe and Aharon were charged with preserving the due honor of the monarchy and speaking with deference to the embattled ruler!

And so they did. Directly prior to the Plague of the Firstborn, Moshe predicts to Pharaoh that in its wake, the Jews will practically be begged to leave: "And all of these ministers of yours will come down to me and prostrate before me, saying, 'Go out!'" (*ibid., 11:8*). Rashi points out that the intended target of this rebuke was really Pharaoh himself, as it was he who ended up seeking out Moshe and not any of his servants. But Moshe purposefully phrased it in this way – "these ministers of yours will come down to me" – as a show of royal respect, so as not to explicitly mention the degradation to the king.

R' Leib Chasman (*ibid.*) articulates the obvious lesson to be gleaned from this episode. How much the more so must we be cautious and respectful in our dealings with our fellow! For aren't all Jews royalty as well? As the Mishnah in Avos (*3:14*) states:

חֲבִיבִין יִשְׂרָאֵל שֶׁנִּקְרְאוּ בָנִים לַמָּקוֹם... שֶׁנֶּאֱמַר בָּנִים אַתֶּם לַה' אֱלֹהֵיכֶם.

"Beloved is Yisrael, for they are referred to as 'Hashem's children'... as it says (*Devarim 14:1*): 'You are sons to Hashem, your G-d.'"

לזכר ולעילוי נשמות

משה בן גרשון הכהן ע"ה

מלכה בת ישראל ע"ה

BO

The Egyptian House of Horrors

Spotlight on Darkness

ONE OF THE EVENTS OF THE *PARSHAH* warranting some added scrutiny is the plague of *choshech* (darkness), which is replete with some unique and intriguing features. Here we will devote specific examination to a particular attribute the *choshech* possessed beyond the "garden variety" darkness:

וַיְהִי חֹשֶׁךְ־אֲפֵלָה בְּכָל־אֶרֶץ מִצְרַיִם שְׁלֹשֶׁת יָמִים. לֹא־רָאוּ אִישׁ אֶת־אָחִיו וְלֹא־קָמוּ אִישׁ מִתַּחְתָּיו שְׁלֹשֶׁת יָמִים וּלְכָל־בְּנֵי יִשְׂרָאֵל הָיָה אוֹר בְּמוֹשְׁבֹתָם.

"And there was thick darkness in all of Egypt for three days. One did not see his fellow, nor did one get up from his place for three days; but all of B'nei Yisrael had light in their dwellings" (Shemos 10:22-23).

Apparently, this darkness was so arresting that not only was the ability of the Mitzrim to see affected, but they were paralyzed as well.

KINDLY TAKE A MOMENT TO STUDY MISHNAS CHAYIM IN THE MERIT OF
DOV *BEN* YEHUDAH LEIB A"H
A FELLOW JEW WHO PASSED AWAY WITH NO RELATIVES TO ARRANGE TORAH STUDY ON BEHALF OF HIS *NESHAMAH*

Why was this added measure of hindering their movements necessary? To a large extent, the imperative was based on the fact that there was a lot taking place behind the scenes throughout the duration of this plague. One of these events was the reconnaissance operation undertaken by the Jews, who retained their vision capabilities. As Rashi points out, while the Mitzrim sat in darkness, B'nei Yisrael scouted around, viewing the valuables of their oppressors and taking inventory. When the time would later come to "relieve" Egypt of its possessions (*cf. Shemos 11:2*), no Mitzri could claim that he did not own this or that item; the Jews knew exactly who had what and where it was stored.

But poking around someone else's house could be a dangerous matter. This idea is brought out in a most dramatic way through the *halachah* of the *ba bamachteres* – the intruder who unlawfully enters a house by tunneling his way in. A householder who discovers such an unwelcome guest is even allowed to eliminate him! As the Mishnah states succinctly (*Sanhedrin 8:6*):

הַבָּא בַּמַּחְתֶּרֶת נִדּוֹן עַל שֵׁם סוֹפוֹ.

"One who intrudes through a tunnel (whose blood is considered forfeit) is so designated based on his (projected) future actions."

The Gemara identifies the safety concerns involved, upon which this seemingly harsh judgment is predicated. An invader is aware that, should he be caught in the act of pilfering, the owner will put up a fight. This is based on the maxim that אֵין אָדָם מַעֲמִיד עַצְמוֹ עַל מָמוֹנוֹ – a person will not restrain himself in the face of a threat to his possessions. The burglar, of course, will respond with force to this attack on his own person. The upshot of this whole arrangement is that any home invader enters with the knowledge and readiness to "neutralize" the homeowner. His "projected future actions" are lethal; and so the homeowner is authorized to preempt the threat on his own life and take out his would-be murderer.

The Maharal (*Gur Aryeh, Shemos 10:23*) understands that the same dynamic was applicable to the situation in Mitzrayim during the Plague of Darkness. Why was it necessary to "freeze" the Egyptians' movements? Recall that the Jews were snooping around their homes at this time. Even if their sight was obstructed, the Egyptians – upon sensing the intruders – would automatically launch into attack mode and harm any Israelite who passed by. To counteract this threat, Hashem visited upon them a darkness that removed not only their vision, but their mobility as well.

Scared of the Dark

WHILE WE NOW UNDERSTAND *WHY* IT WAS necessary to arrest their movements, it still must be explained *how* exactly this was achieved. After all, under regular conditions of darkness, one might have difficulty seeing, but he can still move about!

One way to explain this phenomenon may be to attribute it to the "tangible" nature of this particular darkness. According to the Medrash (*Shemos Rabbah 14:1*), it was as thick as a coin. Perhaps, then, this matter weighed down so heavily upon the Mitzrim that their limbs were simply unable to overcome its density. (One potential difficulty with this explanation, however, is that it may not fully account for their inability to move; after all, the Medrash states merely that the darkness was tactile, but not that it was solid.)

Shedding some light on this topic, the *Hakesav Vehakabbalah* provides an eye-opening approach, which highlights yet another aspect of the Mitzrim's ordeal. He quotes from an apocryphal volume known as "*Chochmas Shlomoh Rabbasi*" (referenced by the Chasam Sofer [*Toras Moshe*] as well), which makes mention of some very interesting occurrences that took place at this time. Apparently, the Mitzrim were actually granted the ability to see certain things during this plague, but this was not for their benefit. In addition to staying in the dark, they were treated to a viewing of some extremely frightening scenes. This was literally an audiovisual horror presentation, in which they heard terrifying sounds and beheld hair-raising visions.

In fact, the *Hakesav Vehakabbalah* attributes one of the familiar phrases of the Pesach Haggadah to this event. In the section recounting the numerous plagues with which the Egyptians were stricken, the Haggadah repeatedly quotes from the verse in Tehillim (88:49): יְשַׁלַּח־בָּם חֲרוֹן אַפּוֹ עֶבְרָה וָזַעַם וְצָרָה מִשְׁלַחַת מַלְאֲכֵי רָעִים – "He sends against them His anger, wrath, fury and torment – a delegation of punitive angels." This "delegation of punitive angels" refers to these celestial messengers who put on for the Mitzrim (sitting in their darkened surroundings) the most terrifying horror show of all time.

In any event, the source for the Mitzrim's arrested mobility seems clear: they were simply frozen in shock. Their harrowing ordeal left them literally paralyzed from fear.

לזכר ולעילוי נשמות
שלמה בן בערל ע"ה
סימא בת צבי הירש ע"ה

BESHALACH

Timely Justice

IF YOU THINK ABOUT IT, THE MAJOR EVENTS OF THE *yetzias* Mitzrayim saga unfold in an unusual way. The Mitzrim's downfall seems to have occurred in two principal stages. First, there are the celebrated ten *makkos*, in which the Egyptians were successively battered by a range of wondrous and destructive forces. These left the land of Egypt virtually devastated and riddled with corpses, compelling Pharaoh to finally capitulate and acquiesce to the Jews' longstanding request to perform service to Hashem in the wilderness.

The destruction, however, was not yet complete. After an intermission of sorts, the final stage is set in motion. This takes place in this week's *parshah*, in which Pharaoh has a change of heart and sets out with his army to pursue B'nei Yisrael. The Mitzrim chase the Jewish people even into the midst of the sea (which had split before them), but – fortunately for us and unfortunately for them – only one nation makes it out alive.

What seems somewhat perplexing is why the process was divided in this manner. Surely, Hashem could have taken care of

---

Kindly take a moment to study Mishnas Chayim in the merit of
Liba *bas* Hershel a"h
a fellow Jew who passed away with no relatives to arrange Torah study on behalf of her *neshamah*

the Mitzrim with the *makkos* alone. Why was the episode "dragged out," so to speak, and the Mitzrim's ultimate destruction delayed? Perhaps the following illustrative story related by the Ben Ish Chai (quoted in *Barchi Nafshi, parshas Beshalach*) can shed some light on the issue:

Cool Under Fire

SOME TIME AGO, A CERTAIN HOUSEHOLDER ASSESSED his desperate financial situation. He simply did not have enough to support his wife and many children, with no bright prospects on the horizon. He decided that, come what may, he must do something to shore up his means.

So he embarked on a journey, travelling far and wide to find adequate employment. Eventually, he discovered a certain bakery concern with which he was able to arrange favorable terms. He was to work in the bakery, but was authorized to take his meals from the plentiful bread and even to sleep on the premises. This meant that he was garnering all profit, with basically no overhead.

After working at this endeavor for a while, he had collected a sizeable sum of earnings; quite enough, he felt, to support his family handsomely for quite some time to come. Gathering his coins into a sack, he loaded up and set out for home.

It was on the road that tragedy struck. An armed bandit appeared out of nowhere, pointing his gun right at the hapless worker. Shaken and deflated, he was forced to hand over his hard-earned fortune.

At this point, his pent-up emotions burst forth. Erupting in tears, he entreated his assailant to just listen for a moment. "Please, I beg you," he intoned. "I have been away from home for so long, working hard to feed my family. What you have taken from me represents the sum total of all of my earnings and the entire fruit of my years of labor. I understand that you will not return it to me. But I have one small thing to ask."

His gun still trained on the victim, the robber considered the petition. No one was around on this abandoned road; he was in no particular rush. "Why not?" he said. "Go ahead and ask."

"The problem is," the man continued, "what to do when I get home. What will my wife say? When she sees me come in empty-handed, she'll think that I wasted my time all of these years!"

"So what do you want from me?" the bandit retorted. "Tell her the truth – you were held up."

"Right," came the reply. "But why would she believe me? I'm just asking if you could furnish me some proof. Let me take off my jacket, and you go ahead and shoot some holes through it. That should convince her of the truth of my statement." In spite of himself, the assailant acquiesced; what did he have to lose? *Bang-bang!*

"And just to complete the picture," the man continued, "let me remove my hat; could you do the same to that?" The bandit obliged. *Bang-bang!* Turning the riddled hat around, the man pressed his luck. "Could you do this side, too?" "But that's it," replied the gunman as he began to pull the trigger.

Click.

That was the sound the man had been waiting for. He quickly jumped on his assailant – whose gun had run out of bullets – and overpowered him, wresting the precious sack from his hands.

Using up the Ammunition

THE EVENTS OF THIS WEEK'S *PARSHAH* CAN BE understood in a similar way, with the aid of some additional background concerning the workings of Hashem's Justice. The Mishnah in Kiddushin (*1:10*) states:

כָּל שֶׁאֵינוֹ עוֹשֶׂה מִצְוָה אַחַת, אֵין מְטִיבִין לוֹ וְאֵין מַאֲרִיכִין לוֹ יָמָיו וְאֵינוֹ נוֹחֵל אֶת הָאָרֶץ.

(Translated literally): "Whoever does not do one mitzvah – will not be treated with benevolence, will not live long and will not inherit the land."

Beshalach / 71

This statement is actually quite complex, subject to much discussion and contains philosophical underpinnings of a very large scope. Here we mention in brief some of the conclusions of the Gemara's interpretation of this passage: The Mishnah speaks of someone whose sins outweigh his merits (such that the performance of another mitzvah would have equalized the tally); and the "benevolence, long life," etc., mentioned here refers to reward in the World to Come. The Mishnah's intent is that such an individual (a *rasha* [wicked person], the majority of whose deeds are sins), will often be accorded success in *this* world, so as to leave him bereft of the bounty of the *Next* World.

Such was Pharaoh's fate, as well. Whereas he underwent quite an ordeal with the *makkos*, his account was not yet liquidated. While certainly qualifying as a *rasha*, he had here and there performed some good deeds in his life. Hashem repays every person for every good deed; and at this point, Pharaoh still had some "ammunition" in his arsenal. His day of final reckoning could not come until these few remaining merits were paid back and used up. His existence and grandeur extended for another few days, until all his shots were expended. Then, his full retribution was at hand.

לזכר ולעילוי נשמת
שמואל יצחק בן הרב נחום דוד ע"ה

YISRO

Privileged Information

R' ITZELE VOLOZHINER – WHO SUCCEEDED HIS father, R' Chaim, as *rosh yeshivah* of Volozhin – often had to appear in the royal halls of power to intercede on behalf of his oppressed brethren. On one of these excursions, he was asked the following by a certain Russian official:

The familiar psalm (*Tehillim 117*) states: הַלְלוּ אֶת־ד׳ כָּל־גּוֹיִם שַׁבְּחוּהוּ כָּל־הָאֻמִּים, כִּי גָבַר עָלֵינוּ חַסְדּוֹ... "Laud Hashem, all nations; praise Him, all peoples; for He has wrought great kindness upon us..." The verse enjoins the nations to praise Hashem. Why? "For He has performed great kindness to *us* (i.e., the Jewish people)!" Is this a satisfactory explanation? The nations of the world should sing Hashem's praises for the kindness He performs for the Jews?

Before proceeding to the answer, let us first explore some fundamental principles regarding Divine Justice. This background will help us to better appreciate R' Itzele's response.

Kindly take a moment to study Mishnas Chayim in the merit of
Yetta Pessil bas Hershel a"h
a fellow Jew who passed away with no relatives to arrange Torah study on behalf of her *neshamah*

THE MISHNAH IN SOTAH (*1:7*) ENCAPSULATES Hashem's method in dealing with His creatures:

Front-Row Seat

בְּמִדָּה שֶׁאָדָם מוֹדֵד, בָּהּ מוֹדְדִין לוֹ.

"According to the measure of a person's actions – that is how Hashem metes out recompense."

This notion of Divine reciprocity is commonly referred to as *midah k'neged midah* (measure for measure). Not only does a person receive reward or punishment for his actions, but the nature of the compensation will resemble the characteristics of the deed. For example, one who dispensed much charity may be blessed with great wealth; a murderer who drowned his victims may very well find himself one day at the bottom of a river (*cf. Avos 2:6*).

This concept was manifest throughout the saga of the Exodus. B'nei Yisrael had for so long languished under the nation that had brutally enslaved them; their Egyptian tormentors devised numerous stratagems to afflict their Hebrew subjects. When the era of retribution arrived, the Jews were able to perceive this aspect of Hashem's justice in the various plagues and punishments that befell their overlords. For example, the Jews had been forced to draw water from the Nile to provide their masters' water needs. When the river turned into blood, it was clearly recognizable how the punishment was fitting: the Mitzrim's entire water supply was neutralized (*R' Bachya*). And so it was with each plague; every detail of the Egyptians' suffering was Divinely calculated to match the nature and magnitude of their nefarious crimes.

However, the Jews' ability to identify the incidences of *midah k'neged midah* had its limitations. The Brisker Rav points out that – while they were able to understand many of the events "plaguing" their former oppressors – there were still numerous times when the *midah k'neged midah* aspect of a particular punishment was less apparent. The reason for their lack of insight was quite understandable; they knew only of the Egyptian decrees that had actually been carried out. But Hashem held the Mitzrim accountable not only for those ideas that came to fruition, but even for those designs that (for one reason or another) never got past the planning stage. Since B'nei Yisrael were never privy to these (aborted) plots, they couldn't know when a Mitzri was receiving punishment that fit his mere evil thoughts.

There was, however, one individual who was capable of noting even these "hidden" aspects of *midah k'neged midah*. This was none other than the protagonist of this week's *parshah* –Yisro. Chazal tell us (*Sotah 11a*) that earlier in his career, Yisro was one of Pharoah's advisers. Before deciding to distance himself from Egypt's rotten scheme, he had been present for the deliberations. As such, he was aware of all parts of the plan, even those that were never implemented. This is one of the reasons he was so shaken and astounded by the events of *yetzias* Mitzrayim. Like no one else, he was able to perceive – down to the last detail – every aspect of Hashem's perfect justice. He recognized how the Egyptians received exact retribution, corresponding not only to their overt actions, but to their hidden designs, as well.

Nocturnal Visit

AGAINST THIS BACKDROP, THE BRISKER RAV supplies R' Itzele's response to the Russian minister: "You thought it strange," R' Itzele explained, "that the gentiles are expected to laud Hashem for the kindness He extends to the Jews. But it is specifically *you* who are most capable of rendering this praise. The Jewish people witness deliverance from their enemies – but only from those threats of which they were aware. Only you know the numerous schemes concocted at the highest levels of power to rain harm upon the Jews – plans that have often been inexplicably thwarted (thanks to Divine protection), but whose details have been suppressed from the public. Who better to praise Hashem for these deliverances than the very ones who promulgated the plots? They are the only witnesses to their failure" (*Chidushei HaGriz al HaTorah; cf. Mishnas Chayim, parshas Tzav, 5770*)!

There is a well-known incident to this effect, recorded not only in the sacred volumes, but in the archives of Czarist Russia. The event centered upon the activities of the notoriously anti-Semitic Czar Nikolai, who was indefatigable in his efforts to persecute his Jewish subjects. Czar Nikolai expended much time and toil devising harsh decrees aimed at decimating the Jews.

But he began to notice something. It seemed that each time, at the conclusion of a parliamentary session dedicated to the formulation of these wicked decrees, the matter would somehow be dropped. An extensive private investigation uncovered that intervention – and some well-placed bribes from Jewish activists – were responsible for curtailing his ministers' effectiveness.

Czar Nikolai decided to stave off this "rail-roading" once and for all. He convened his officials and issued strict instructions. This time, the ministers were to work on the anti-Jewish legislation throughout the night; they could not even leave the hall. To ensure compliance, Czar Nikolai announced that he would personally appear at 3:00 in the morning to sign the decree.

The ministers were quite surprised at 2:00 a.m. by a sudden commotion; it seemed that the Czar and his royal entourage had chosen to make an inspection one hour before the deadline. Imagine their surprise when the Czar picked up the documents and tore them to shreds before their very eyes! After this bewildering and quite visible spectacle, the ministers understood that it was time to call it quits, and home they went.

The Czar appeared, as scheduled, at 3:00 a.m., eager to sign the long-awaited decree. But he was astounded by what he found: an empty parliament building! After conferring with the few attendant guards who remained, he was apprised of the unlikely events: apparently, some likeness of the Czar himself had just one hour earlier come and destroyed the legislation.

Shocked and dismayed, the Czar was heard to mutter: "The G-d of Israel neither sleeps nor slumbers" (*She'al Avicha V'yagedcha*, I, 301-2).

לזכר ולעילוי נשמת
מלכה ע"ה בת שלום נ"י

MISHPATIM

Every Dog Has His (Sabbath) Day

The following is based primarily on R' Yitzchak Zilberstein's accounts as recorded in the sefer V'ha'arev Na, Vol. 3 (*parshas Mishpatim*).

THE MAN KNEW THAT IT WOULD BE A WINDFALL FOR his friend, a very recent *ba'al teshuvah*. As the driver slated to take R' Chaim Kanievsky to a *simchah* in Yerushalayim the following day, he invited his friend to come along for this once-in-a-lifetime opportunity: a full hour sitting next to the venerated sage. The guest would have him practically all to himself, to ask whatever he pleased.

In the car the next day, the eager (but novice) "student" got right down to business. He posed his first question to R' Chaim: "We have recently become observant and are slowly learning about the *mitzvos*. Our family has just started reciting Kiddush on Shabbos night. My question is: We have a dog that is most loyal and beloved, almost a member of the family. Does he also have to hear Kiddush?"

KINDLY TAKE A MOMENT TO STUDY MISHNAS CHAYIM IN THE MERIT OF
ROCHEL BAS YEHUDAH A"H
A FELLOW JEW WHO PASSED AWAY WITH NO RELATIVES TO ARRANGE TORAH STUDY ON BEHALF OF HER *NESHAMAH*

"There is definitely room for leniency here," R' Chaim answered patiently.

The questioner went right on to his next issue: "Concerning the *halachah* that one may not eat before he has fed his animals (*Berachos 40a*), does this apply to a pet dog, as well?"

"For this," the sage answered, "one should be stringent."

By this point, R' Chaim realized which way the wind was blowing (insofar as the content of today's questions was concerned). As a towering Torah figure, R' Chaim scrupulously avoids any hint of time-wasting activity. On the other hand, this great sage was equally mindful and concerned with the feelings of his eager companion.

To accommodate both concerns, R' Chaim came up with an idea. He turned to his son (who had accompanied them on the journey) and initiated a "game" of sorts. "Let's see," R' Chaim explained, "where does Talmud Bavli make mention of 'dogs?'"

And that is how they spent the remainder of the trip: Listing all of the places in maseches Berachos in which dogs are mentioned; then Shabbos; then Eruvin, etc.

Purina... for Shalosh Se'udos

THIS LATTER ISSUE (OF PLACING FOOD FIRST BEFORE one's animal) actually carries some interesting ramifications with regard to Shabbos observance. The details emerge from a Mishnah that outlines the proper conduct in the event of a fire breaking out on Shabbos (when all persons have been properly evacuated and there is only a danger to property). The owner is only permitted to salvage a limited quantity of food from the premises, as the Mishnah states (*Shabbos 16:2*):

מַצִּילִין מְזוֹן שָׁלֹשׁ סְעֻדּוֹת - הָרָאוּי לְאָדָם לְאָדָם, הָרָאוּי לַבְּהֵמָה לַבְּהֵמָה. כֵּיצַד. נָפְלָה דְלֵקָה בְּלֵילֵי שַׁבָּת, מַצִּילִין מְזוֹן שָׁלֹשׁ סְעֻדּוֹת, בַּשַּׁחֲרִית, מַצִּילִין מְזוֹן שְׁתֵּי סְעֻדּוֹת, בַּמִּנְחָה, מְזוֹן סְעֻדָּה אֶחָת.

> "One may salvage three meals' worth of food: "people-worthy" food for people and animal food for one's animals. The actual amount may fluctuate: If the fire breaks out (at the beginning of) Shabbos night, then one salvages three meals' worth (for the meals yet to come on Shabbos); if it breaks out in the morning, one salvages only enough food for the two remaining meals; in the afternoon, one salvages only enough for the one remaining meal (shalosh se'udos)."

The Tiferes Yisrael makes a salient observation. In speaking here of the amount deemed essential for proper Shabbos enjoyment – i.e., three meals' worth – the Mishnah refers to both humans *and animals*. Since when are animals obligated to eat three meals on Shabbos like their human masters?

It must be, he concludes, that the Mishnah was mindful of the *halachah* mentioned above – namely, that *before* one sits down to enjoy a meal, he must serve food to his animals. The Tiferes Yisrael's approach would give rise to a most curious practice. A dog may be accustomed to one meal a day. But when it comes to Shabbos, "Fido" is eligible for the same three Shabbos meals as the rest of the family (although exempt from Kiddush; see above).

The matter can actually be taken one step further. Not only is a pet owner encouraged (based on the above) to supply his animal with three square Shabbos meals, he may even be enjoined to provide higher quality fare in reflection of the special day.

When mentioning the Sabbath day, the verse in this week's *parshah* states: "On the seventh day you shall cease work, so that your ox and your mule may rest" (*Shemos 23:12*). Rashi comments that the intent of the verse is to charge the owner with ensuring that his animals are given an opportunity to attain a measure of Shabbos pleasure of their own. Accordingly, the Chavos Yair records the practice of a certain pious individual who would supply his animals with an extra bountiful portion on Shabbos, so that they, too, could experience their "*Shabbos mechayeh*" (*Mekor Chaim, Kitzur Halachos §246*).

R' Yitzchak Zilberstein was asked a question by a recent *ba'al teshuvah* who was also a dog-owner. He was thinking of serving his dog more expensive (tastier?) dog food on Shabbos but was unsure if this was a completely mistaken notion. Based on the above, R' Yitzchak demonstrated that there may be a place for *oneg Shabbos* (experiencing special Shabbos delight) – even for dogs.

לזכר ולעילוי נשמת
יעקב בן לוי ע"ה

TERUMAH

Who are the Leviim?

THE RAMBAM FAMOUSLY STATES THAT (IN SOME sense, at least) membership in that select class of elevated Jews known as "Leviim" is not necessarily restricted to those of Levite lineage. After providing a laudatory description of the Leviim's status – how they are excluded from receiving an inheritance in Eretz Yisroel so that they will be completely immersed in Hashem's service and in the preservation and teaching of His Laws to the nation – the Rambam clarifies to whom else this designation is applied:

"And it is not the Tribe of Levi alone, but any person... who is moved by his expansive spirit... to entirely dedicate himself to Hashem's Service... and study of His Word... and casts off from himself the yoke of the pursuit of the masses... such an individual becomes sanctified... Hashem will be his portion and inheritance for eternity and will ensure that even in this world he will be granted sufficient sustenance, just as He apportioned gifts (such as tithes) to the Kohanim and Leviim" (*Hilchos Shemitah V'yoveil 13:13*).

Kindly take a moment to study Mishnas Chayim in the merit of

Leib ben Meir a"h

a fellow Jew who passed away with no relatives to arrange Torah study on behalf of his *neshamah*

Bearers of the Aron Kodesh (Holy Ark)

THE CHAFETZ CHAIM PICKS UP THIS THREAD. THIS week's *parshah* spells out the details of the *Mishkan* (Tabernacle) and the arrangement of its various components and areas. The outer perimeter area, known as the *Chatzer* (courtyard), surrounded the *Mishkan*. The *Mishkan* itself, of more sacred quality, was comprised mainly of the *Heichal* (sanctuary), which led to the most restricted area – the *Kodesh Hakodashim* ("Holy of Holies"). This most sacred chamber housed the *Aron Hakodesh*, within which resided the very Word of Hashem, inscribed on the *Luchos* (stone tablets handed to Moshe on Har Sinai). It was the Leviim's charge to protect the sanctity of these areas from unauthorized entry (especially the Holy Ark in the innermost chamber), and, of course, from any ritual defilement. Thus, the Leviim were conferred with the prestigious title of שׁוֹמְרֵי מִשְׁמֶרֶת הַקֹּדֶשׁ – "Keepers of the Sacred Charge" (*Bamidbar 3:28*).

So, too, there are individuals who serve as modern-day שׁוֹמְרֵי מִשְׁמֶרֶת הַקֹּדֶשׁ. These are the *talmidei chachamim*, whose dedication to the Torah – its teachings and principles – places them in the position of preserving its sanctity and dignity. They stand in the vanguard against those who seek to defile, dilute or distort its sacred words. In fact, in some respects, they are even greater than the original Leviim. The Leviim had the coveted task of Bearers of the *Aron Hakodesh*; but this was at a time when Hashem's Sanctuary was in full function, and His Glory was openly revealed and acknowledged. Today, with the absence of a *Mikdash* and the concealment of Hashem's Presence in the world, the *talmidei chachamim's* job is that much harder. They seek to defend the Torah's honor within a climate of cynicism, often encountering much hostility in the process. Thus, the Chafetz Chaim asserts, they should not view themselves as objects worthy of scorn, *chas v'Shalom*; rather, they are today's Bearers of the *Aron Hakodesh*, occupying a place of esteem rivaling that of the Leviim of the Temple (*Shem Olam, Sha'ar His'chazkus, ch. 2, second footnote*).

Delicate Balance

INDEED, THOSE WHO DEDICATE THEMSELVES TO a life of Torah study must perform a delicate balancing act. As we have just seen, they truly stand at the forefront of the nation and should consider themselves as such. On the other hand, the amassment of great stores of Torah knowledge should not be a stumbling block to conceit. While appreciating the magnitude of his value and position, the proper Torah scholar is careful that his accomplishments do not "go to his head." As the Mishnah states so succinctly (*Pirkei Avos 2:9*):

אִם לָמַדְתָּ תּוֹרָה הַרְבֵּה, אַל תַּחֲזִיק טוֹבָה לְעַצְמָךְ, כִּי לְכָךְ נוֹצָרְתָּ.

> "If you have learned much Torah, do not attribute undue greatness to yourself; because (you are merely fulfilling the mission) for which you were created."

This concept is manifest as well in one of the most remarkable features of the *Aron Hakodesh*. The *Aron* was 2 ½ cubits long. It was placed in the middle of the Holy of Holies, which had a width of 20 cubits. Thus, if one were to measure from either side of the *Aron* to the side walls of the Holy of Holies, he should obtain a reading of 8 ¾ cubits (20 − 2½ = 17½ ÷ 2 = 8¾). But, the *Gemara* tells us, if one would actually perform this measuring exercise, he would find that there were exactly 10 cubits on each side! In other words, while it was 2½ cubits long, the *Aron Hakodesh* actually took up *no physical space* (*Yoma 21a and Rashi there*). (We hope to elaborate more on this concept in the coming weeks, *Be'ezras Hashem*).

What was said so far concerned the *Aron Hakodesh*; what about the *Luchos* themselves, which rested inside? One may have assumed that this quality surely applied to them as well. If the *Aron Hakodesh*, the vessel that housed the *Luchos*, was itself so "spiritual" that it would not register on the physical scale, then certainly the tablets themselves, which were even more sacred, would be beyond the range of physical tracking.

Yet, this was not the case. This is apparent from the Gemara in Bava Basra (*14a*), which makes precise calculations concerning how the *Luchos* fit and rested within the confines of the *Aron*.

To what can we attribute this phenomenon, by which the *Aron* was not constricted by space, but the *Luchos* themselves were subject to physical properties? R' Moshe Feinstein (*Darash Moshe*) sees therein a poignant lesson, along the lines of our discussion above:

A *talmid chacham* must conduct himself like the *Aron Hakodesh*; that is, just as the *Aron* contained Hashem's teachings (inscribed on the *Luchos*), so, too, the Torah scholar is responsible for housing Hashem's Torah within himself. As such, he must be fluent in the entirety of Torah, to the extent that he is *completely filled* with Torah knowledge, which permeates every area of his being. Any portion of the breadth and depth of Torah that he neglects to attain represents "wasted space" and unused capacity.

At the same time, however, he cannot be goaded to undue haughtiness because of his singular achievements. As a holding vessel for the Torah, he is a living *Aron Hakodesh*. A surefire way to retain ample humility would be to bear in mind what the Gemara in *Yoma* reveals about the Ark's properties: אָרוֹן אֵינוֹ מִן הַמִּדָה – "The *Aron* has no dimensions" (in terms of taking up space). This is a stark reminder for the ideal way in which to conduct oneself – keeping small, as if one has no dimensions at all.

לזכר ולעילוי נשמת

חיים אריה בן יצחק ע"ה

TETZAVEH

A Fitting Crown

The Kohein-King Connection

THERE APPEAR TO BE CERTAIN PARALLELS BETWEEN the *Kohein Gadol* (High Priest) and the *melech* (king), which can be derived from this week's *parshah*. Perhaps the most obvious of these is the general theme of *kavod* (honor). This is the thrust of the special priestly garments the *Kohein Gadol* and his priestly offspring were to don – לְכָבוֹד וּלְתִפְאָרֶת – "for honor and glory" (*Shemos 28:2,40*). Of course, the honor due the *melech* is likewise a key component of the nation's interactions with their monarch. We find numerous *halachos* (laws) aimed at protecting his honor and preserving his dignity. As the Mishnah states (*Sanhedrin 2:8*):

אֵין רוֹכְבִין עַל סוּסוֹ, וְאֵין יוֹשְׁבִין עַל כִּסְאוֹ, וְאֵין מִשְׁתַּמְּשִׁין בְּשַׁרְבִיטוֹ, וְאֵין רוֹאִין אוֹתוֹ כְּשֶׁהוּא מִסְתַּפֵּר וְלֹא כְשֶׁהוּא עָרוֹם וְלֹא בְּבֵית הַמֶּרְחָץ, שֶׁנֶּאֱמַר שׂוֹם תָּשִׂים עָלֶיךָ מֶלֶךְ, שֶׁתְּהֵא אֵימָתוֹ עָלֶיךָ.

> KINDLY TAKE A MOMENT TO STUDY MISHNAS CHAYIM IN THE MERIT OF
> **YA'AKOV BEN LOUIS A"H**
> A FELLOW JEW WHO PASSED AWAY WITH NO RELATIVES TO ARRANGE TORAH STUDY ON BEHALF OF HIS *NESHAMAH*

> "No one (aside from the king) may ride his personal horse, sit in his seat, nor use his scepter. One may not view him while he takes a haircut, is without clothing, or in the bath-house; as is mandated by the verse, 'You shall place the king on you' (Devarim 17:15), intimating that his awe should be upon you."

A more specific item shared by these two figures is the crown. This has an obvious manifestation in the case of the king, but the head of the *Kohein Gadol* is similarly bedecked. One of his unique vestments is the *Tzitz*, the golden plate that adorns his head; this is referred to by the verse as the *"nezer hakodesh"* (crown of sanctity) (*Shemos* 39:30).

This *Tzitz*-crown connection can be the source of some fascinating insights. We shall hopefully discover this after laying some preliminary groundwork.

Heads Up

ONE ITEM WE NEED TO CLARIFY BEFORE proceeding further is the issue of head shapes. The first thing that ordinarily pops into mind (no pun intended) when contemplating head shapes is roundness. In crude stick-figure drawings, for instance, the "stick" is usually topped by a circle-shaped ball.

But closer inspection reveals that assigning mere "roundness" to the average head is a less than accurate portrayal. Few people have a globe perched on top of their necks. To be more precise, a head is generally appointed by a flatter facial area (barring noses or other protuberances) culminating in a forehead; the remaining hair-covered head area above and behind is what accounts for the quality of roundness. Stated another way, the letter "D" might be a more faithful representative of head shape than the letter "O."

Now, this arrangement might present some challenge when it comes to donning a crown. By and large, these precious-metal objects resemble a large, circular ring. As such, they might actually do better if placed on a ball-shaped head than upon the conventional "D" model.

One seemingly simple way to "circumvent" the problem would be to simply place the crown on the top/back part of the head that retains a round shape. This might be the ideal solution for *gentile* kings; as we shall soon see, however, the matter is not that simple as far as the Israelite kings are concerned.

Perfect Fit

THE COMPLICATION THAT ARISES HAS TO DO WITH the *tefillin shel rosh* (*tefillin* worn on the head), which are supposed to be placed between the hairline and the "soft-spot" on the upper portion of the head (*Menachos 37a*). Let us return briefly to the headwear of the *Kohein Gadol*. As mandated in this week's *parshah*, the *Kohein Gadol* had to don both the *Tzitz* and the *Mitznefes* (turban-like headdress). In addition to all of this, he also had to find space for his *tefillin*! The Gemara (*Archin 3b*) states that a shock of hair was actually visible between the *Mitznefes* on top and the *Tzitz* below. That is where the *tefillin* were to be placed – on the spot directly above the *Tzitz*. And while this might sound a bit tight, there is actually just enough room here for the *tefillin*. The Gemara states (*Avodah Zarah 44a*) that there is enough room on the front of the head to provide for two pairs of head *tefillin* (one on top of the other). Similarly, it could accommodate a *Tzitz* with *tefillin* right above it.

Let us recall also that the *Tzitz* is a type of crown. And so, the *Toras Chaim* explains (*Avodah Zarah, ibid.*), this is where the crown-problem arises. The *melech* was to wear his crown in the same place as the *Tzitz* – that is, right below where the *tefillin* would rest. In other words, he could not wear his circle-shaped crown on the upper, round part of his head, but had to place it around his hair-line area – a basically level region. What to do? The only way his round crown could fit properly and snuggly on this flat surface would be by some miracle.

Which is exactly what happened. The Gemara in Avodah Zarah (*ibid.*) states that one of the hallmarks of the Davidic dynasty was that the crowns they used would fit only on their heads, but not on the head of any pretender to the throne. Tosafos explains that the reference here is to the aforementioned miracle – that the circular crown fit perfectly on the non-round area of their heads.

Incidentally, it is interesting to note that the words of the popular song have their roots in this dissertation. Why, indeed, did the Davidic kings employ these round crowns (which could only fit with a miracle)? The *Toras Chaim* explains that the circular shape – symbolizing a continuum – reflects the fact that David Hamelech's dynasty will exist in perpetuity. He concludes with the fitting quote from the Gemara in Rosh Hashanah (*25a*) – דָּוִד מֶלֶךְ יִשְׂרָאֵל חַי וְקַיָּם – *David, King of Yisrael, lives on!*

לזכר ולעילוי נשמות
נחמן שמעון בן יהודה מאיר הכהן ע״ה
מלכה אלטע בת יחיאל מיכל הכהן ע״ה

KI SISA

The Thin Line

An exposition of the mystifying event known as the "Cheit Ha'eigel" – Sin of the Golden Calf.

WE HAVE PREVIOUSLY DISCUSSED THE UNIQUE property of the *Aron Hakodesh* (Holy Ark), which was "beyond the realm of measurement"; that is, it did not take up any physical space within the *Kodesh Hakadashim* – the Holy of Holies, the chamber wherein it resided. While it quite difficult for us to conceptualize, additional insight into this phenomenon may actually be gleaned by examining a central theme of this week's *parshah* – the episode of the *Cheit Ha'eigel*.

THE GREAT TORAH TEACHERS THROUGHOUT the generations have been perplexed by this seemingly inexplicable event. How could a nation – who had witnessed the miracles of the Exodus, and were standing by the very mountain where they beheld Hashem's Presence and heard Him prohibit the practice of idolatry – turn around, fashion a golden calf, and proclaim "This took us out of Egypt"?!

An Image Problem

Kindly take a moment to study Mishnas Chayim in the merit of
Yehudis bas Yosef a"h
A fellow Jew who passed away with no relatives to arrange Torah study on behalf of her *Neshamah*

Indeed, a significant body of commentators relate that, despite appearances, the deed was actually bereft of idolatrous intent. To provide a thorough and complete explanation of exactly what the act *did* entail is way beyond the scope of this article. For our immediate purposes, we make brief mention here of one approach, advanced by the Kuzari (*I:27*) and R' Yehonasan Eibschutz (*Tiferes Yehonasan*). They contend that, while a grievous error, the idea of the Golden Calf *seemed* to have had precedent, and from an authorized source. At first glance, the notion is not so far off from the *Keruvim* on the *Aron Kodesh* – the angelic, golden figurines which adorned the cover of this sacred vessel.

It is worth noting further where these *Keruvim* were housed. Consider the following Mishnah, which discusses the proper directional alignment for prayer. The Mishnah states (*Berachos 4:5*):

הָיָה רוֹכֵב עַל הַחֲמוֹר, יֵרֵד. וְאִם אֵינוֹ יָכוֹל לֵירֵד, יַחֲזִיר אֶת פָּנָיו, וְאִם אֵינוֹ יָכוֹל לְהַחֲזִיר אֶת פָּנָיו, יְכַוֵּן אֶת לִבּוֹ כְּנֶגֶד בֵּית קֹדֶשׁ הַקֳּדָשִׁים.

"If someone was riding a donkey (when the time for prayer arrives), he should (stop and) descend (to pray). If he is unable to descend, he should (at least) turn his face (towards the direction soon to be mentioned). If he is unable (even) to turn his face, he should (at least) direct his heart towards the Kodesh Hakadashim."

The *Kodesh Hakadashim* effectively serves as the Gates to Heaven, as all Yisrael directs their prayers towards this hallowed location. It is appropriately considered the most sacred area in the world – the "Holy of Holies". And what is placed right in the midst of this holiest of places, to which only the High Priest may access, on the holiest day of the year? What is contained directly behind the partition, sitting directly in the line of the prayers of all Yisrael? Two molten, golden images.

And so, the question practically begs itself: How, exactly, is this arrangement sanctioned? Doesn't the Torah repeatedly condemn any suggestion of or resemblance to idolatry? Doesn't it explicitly forbid the crafting and keeping of such images, even where no express idolatry is involved; as the verse states (*Shemos 20:20*): "Do not make... images of silver, or images of gold..."!

S OME COMMENTATORS CONTEND, IN FACT, THAT the fashioning of the *Keruvim* should, inherently, fall within the purview of the aforementioned prohibition. They explain this is

To the Letter one other example of those unique *halachic* instances wherein the Torah itself inserts an exception to an otherwise binding restriction (known in Talmudic terminology as "*hutar michlalo*"). A sister-in-law is included in the Torah's list of illicit marriages (i.e., one may not wed a woman who was formerly married to his brother). The exception arises in the case of levirate marriage ("*yibum*"); where the brother died childless, the surviving brother is then *supposed* to marry the widow, to produce offspring to uphold the name of the deceased. Similarly, crafting molten images is normally proscribed, yet it is a mitzvah to fashion the *Keruvim* for the *Aron* and place them in the *Kodesh Hakadashim* (*Derashos Mahari Mintz*, referenced in *K'motzei Shalal Rav, parshas Terumah*).

What emerges from this idea is the imperative to simply follow instructions. Someone fashioning the *Keruvim* may be moved to make them out of silver instead of gold, or to make four instead of two. But if he does so, explains Rashi (*Shemos, ibid.*), he immediately incurs a violation of the prohibition against images. If he follows the Torah's guidelines, he performs a great *mitzvah*; if he deviates based on his own predilections, he is rendered a transgressor. (*Cf. Meshech Chochmah, Shemos 37:1*).

The above discussion may provide us with at least some minimal insight regarding the *Cheit Ha'eigel*. As noted, their act was not some wanton, random frenzy to suddenly embrace idolatry. Rather, the deed was intended as Divine Service, resembling, in spirit, the idea of the *Keruvim*. However, they were missing a key element; as the Beis Halevi explains, they acted from their own initiative, without a command from Hashem. Their intentions may have been pristine, but in an area such as this, one walks a very thin line. A slight deviation from Divine Guidance may mean the difference between a meritorious deed and a grievous misstep.

R' Ya'akov Kamenetsky explains (*Emes L'Ya'akov, Shemos 20:20*) that this could be the lesson of the *Aron*'s wondrous feature. This vessel, containing the *Keruvim*, was not detectable, as far as normative measurement is concerned. This is a phenomenon which finite, human comprehension can not fully grasp. But this was specifically the Torah's intent: to highlight the imperative of dedicating our minds and hearts solely to Hashem's Word. Reliance on one's own (limited) intellect to fully unravel the secret of the *Keruvim* is a futile and even dangerous exercise; as we have seen, those who thought along these lines were led astray. In this and all areas, the guiding principle should not be our personal conceptions, but what Hashem Himself has prescribed.

לזכר ולעילוי נשמת
הרב יעקב בן ניסן זצ"ל

VAYAKHEL

Plenty of Room

IN PREVIOUS WEEKS WE HAVE DISCUSSED the curious quality of the *Aron Hakodesh* (Holy Ark) to literally sit in a room without taking up any space; this, despite the fact that it was actually comprised of two-and-a-half cubits of solid gold-plated wood. (In other words, if one was to measure the room before the *Aron* was placed inside of it and then repeat the process again after placing the *Aron* inside [this time measuring from either side of the *Aron* to the walls], one would arrive at the same figure.) Such a phenomenon reflected the inherently spiritual nature of this sacred vessel, which was apparently unbounded by the usual restrictions of natural laws and dimensions.

THE TRUTH OF THE MATTER IS THAT THIS characteristic was not limited to the *Aron*; in fact, it was a feature of the *Mikdash* (Sanctuary) in general. As this *parshah* continues with the Sanctuary theme, we are afforded the opportunity to further examine the wondrous nature of this entity.

Close Quarters

KINDLY TAKE A MOMENT TO STUDY MISHNAS CHAYIM IN THE MERIT OF
ELIEZER *BEN* MENASHE *A"H*
A FELLOW JEW WHO PASSED AWAY WITH NO RELATIVES TO ARRANGE TORAH STUDY ON BEHALF OF HIS *NESHAMAH*

Three times a year, during the pilgrimage festivals, the entire Jewish nation would visit the *Mikdash* site. While this was a beautiful display of unity and a sight to behold, the mass convergence of worshippers into one area presented a logistical issue: namely, how could the throngs fit together with any level of comfort? Furthermore, with the entire nation suddenly arriving from distant points all over the country, imagine the motel rooms necessary to fit everyone; finding proper accommodations must have been a national nightmare.

And yet, the Mishnah tells us, both of these issues were addressed and solved in a miraculous fashion. Indeed, the situation inside the Sanctuary was quite "compact"; the Bartenura (*Avos 5:5*) cites that as they stood together in prayer, the congregation was so tightly packed together that, for many, their feet literally did not touch the ground as they remained suspended between their neighbors. When it was time to prostrate, one would have imagined that the simultaneous bowing exercise of such a multitude would be impossible. The Mishnah (*ibid.*) tells us otherwise, as it sheds light on this and the other space-related challenge mentioned above:

עֲשָׂרָה נִסִּים נַעֲשׂוּ לַאֲבוֹתֵינוּ בְּבֵית הַמִּקְדָּשׁ... עוֹמְדִים צְפוּפִים וּמִשְׁתַּחֲוִים רְוָחִים... וְלֹא אָמַר אָדָם לַחֲבֵרוֹ צַר לִי הַמָּקוֹם שֶׁאָלִין בִּירוּשָׁלָיִם.

"Ten miracles were wrought for our forefathers in the Beis Hamikdash... They would stand packed together, but bow with plenty of room... and no one ever complained to his friend that he was unable to find proper lodging within Yerushalayim."

Once again we find the *Mikdash* area seeming to defy the laws of nature and the confines of physical space. Despite the inundation of guests, there was always a place to stay. And despite a crowded prayer hall, there was plenty of room to bow down. In fact, the Bartenura (*ibid.*) adds that upon bowing, each worshipper suddenly found himself with his own personal space, separated from his neighbors by four cubits. (Remember that a moment before he was literally suspended in midair, pressed between the shoulders of his fellow *daveners*.)

The Seasonal Exchange

THE FEATURE DESCRIBED ABOVE HAS SOME far-reaching ramifications and may even be the source of a puzzling aspect of one of Klal Yisrael's time-honored and cherished customs.

While the *regalim* (pilgrimage festivals of Pesach, Shavuos, and Sukkos) are anticipated and appreciated by all, there is an associated ritual that holds particular meaning for those individuals whose parents, unfortunately, are no longer with them. This holds true even for many less affiliated Jews; when this time of year comes around, the synagogue pews become filled with those seeking to recite the Yizkor prayer, in which their loved ones are commemorated.

The perplexing aspect of this practice is that, at first glance, it appears somewhat incongruous with the season. Yizkor is a solemn occasion, evoking much emotion for the participants. Why, then, is *yom tov* considered an acceptable time to engage in this practice? The order and mitzvah of the day is *simchah* (joy); Yizkor recital, while important, tends to conjure up a certain sentimental solemnity. Shouldn't a different day be set aside for fulfilling this custom? What is the connection to the *regalim* specifically?

The Kav Hayashar, a *mussar* classic replete with mystical themes in addition to ethical exhortations, provides a most fascinating explanation on this issue, invoking the "*mishtachavim rechavim*" (expansive prostration) concept mentioned above. Not only does he brilliantly utilize this idea to present a solution, but he also sheds much light on the "mechanics" responsible for the facilitation of this marvelous occurrence.

Chazal refer frequently to the existence of two (simultaneous) *Batei Mikdash*: the *Beis Hamikdash Shel Matah* (Lower, or Earthly Temple) and the *Beis Hamikdash Shel Ma'alah* (Upper, Celestial Temple). The (Earthly) *Beis Hamikdash*, when it stood, was obviously a most sacred entity. But imagine, in comparison, the *kedushah* (holiness) infused in the *Beis Hamikdash Shel Ma'alah*; its spiritual magnitude is of a level completely unfathomable to mortal man. Nevertheless, there is some parity between these two "edifices," as they function in tandem, to a certain extent.

Thus, an interesting occurrence would take place during the *regalim*, when the Jewish nation would make their pilgrimage to the site of the *Mikdash Shel Matah*. Simultaneously, a "visit" of sorts would be undertaken in the Celestial spheres, as the Jews' forebears – Avraham, Yitzchak, and Ya'akov – would pay homage in the *Mikdash Shel Ma'alah*.

The forefathers' arrival at "their" *Mikdash* site activated a phenomenal event: the *Mikdash Shel Ma'alah* would actually descend to and (temporarily) take the place of the *Mikdash Shel Matah*, so that the Jewish people were now actually stationed within the *Mikdash Shel Ma'alah*. It was the heightened spiritual atmosphere, contends the Kav Hayashar, that was thus responsible for the release from the bonds of physics, allowing the crowded worshippers to prostrate themselves with ample, newfound space.

This forms the basis, the Kav Hayashar concludes, of linking the Yizkor service specifically with the *regalim*. Since this remarkable chain of events was effected by the visit of our forefathers to the Celestial Temple during the festival period, we invoke their memory then, together with the memories of more immediate forebears, and pray for all to merit a favorable remembrance.

לזכר ולעילוי נשמות
דוד בן ברוך שלום ע"ה
גיטל רחל בת בונים מנחם מנדל ע"ה

PEKUDEI

A Mountain on Top of a Hair

Big Things in Small Packages

WHEN CONTEMPLATING THE IMMENSITY OF THE scope of wisdom contained in the Torah, we are awestruck not only by its vastness, but by the unusual phenomenon that so much is contained within such little space. Consider, for example, the statement of the Mishnah in Chagigah (*1:8*) concerning a number of large bodies in *halachah*:

> הִלְכוֹת שַׁבָּת חֲגִיגוֹת וְהַמְעִילוֹת, הֲרֵי הֵם כַּהֲרָרִים הַתְּלוּיִין בְּשַׂעֲרָה, שֶׁהֵן מִקְרָא מְעָט וַהֲלָכוֹת מְרֻבּוֹת.

> "The halachos of Shabbos, chagigos (specialized festival offerings) and me'ilos (laws governing the unauthorized usage of sanctified objects) are like mountains suspended upon a strand of hair; that is, their particulars are numerous, but they are derived from the briefest of scriptural references."

Kindly take a moment to study Mishnas Chayim in the merit of
Otto *ben* Julius *a"h*
a fellow Jew who passed away with no relatives to arrange Torah study on behalf of his *neshamah*

For the moment, let us just focus on the first of these three items. Maseches Shabbos, in *mishnayos*, contains more chapters (twenty-four) than almost any other tractate. The Gemara volume likewise contains more *blatt* (folios) than almost any other (157). Over 100 *simanim* in Shulchan Aruch are devoted merely to recording the final, conclusive *halachic* decisions of this area of observance. And how many commentaries, responsa and other *sefarim* have been produced over the centuries to further clarify the many crucial Shabbos issues? It is not uncommon to find numerous works covering a single *melachah* (form of labor) or even just a subsection of a single *melachah*! And a substantial portion of this huge mountain of thousands or millions of pages worth of material covering this subject can be traced backed to a nuanced phrase or an extra letter in the biblical text.

The Chafetz Chaim elaborates on this theme (*Shem Olam, Sha'ar Hachzakas HaTorah, ch. 12, first footnote*). Anyone somewhat familiar with Talmud study immediately understands the connotation conveyed by a reference to the three "*Bava*"s: Bava Kamma, Bava Metzia and Bava Basra. Each of these individually, and all three collectively, comprise a body of intricate legal law known both for its volume and complexity. True mastery of this material requires years of intense and diligent study. Yet, one Shabbos, we go to *shul* and listen to the public Torah reading of *parshas* Mishpatim. There, within the course of a few minutes, we hear the *pesukim* that are the foundation of basically all of the aforementioned material! During *parshas* Ki Seitzei, the reader chants the section beginning with "*Ki yikach ish ishah*" (When a man takes a woman) (*Devarim 24:1*). After four verses, he has covered what is for the most part the entire biblical basis of another two great and weighty tractates – Gittin and Kiddushin (dealing with divorce and marriage).

Let us bear in mind that it is not only overt ritual law, but all areas of knowledge, that are contained in the Torah, also often from relatively short passages. The Chafetz Chaim goes on to demonstrate how a great part of the discipline of astronomy is rooted in the study of *kiddush hachodesh* (sanctification of the new moon, including the intricacies of intercalation), surgical/anatomical principles emerge from a Mishnah in Ohalos (*end of chapter 1*), geometry and complex mathematical measuring is contained in Maseches Kilayim (*chapters 3, 5*), etc.

Celestial Blueprint

IT IS IN THE CONTEXT OF THIS DISCUSSION THAT WE now turn our focus to the current *parshiyos*. In light of the above, the *parshiyos* of Vayakhel and Pekudei, at first glance, seem all the more perplexing. As we have seen, the Torah put a great premium on space, in that huge mountains of wisdom are contained within extremely small samplings of the sacred text – "mountains leaning on a hairsbreadth." *Parshas* Terumah and *parshas* Tetzaveh record, in significant detail, the instructions to fashion the Sanctuary and its implements, as well as the priestly garments (respectively). Seemingly, the Torah could have appended two words to these sections: – וַיַּעֲשׂוּ כֵן – (and they did so), and that would be that. Instead, however, the Torah devotes two entire *parshiyos* recounting – individually and at length – how each of the instructions was carried out: "And they made the curtains... thirty-one cubits long... fifty loops on the edge... and they made the boards... and Betzalel made the Ark... the Menorah... they made the Breastplate... with gold, blue, purple... the robe... etc. How can we account for what appears as a major departure from the usual pattern of funneling maximum data into minimal text?

The truth is that the Torah is really filled with boundless wisdom, including a store of breathtaking, timeless secrets. For example, the Vilna Gaon states that every single moment of the lives and history of every single living creature and inanimate object is contained within the Torah's words; if one was able to plumb its depths, one could uncover the details of every single moment of one's (or anyone or anything else's) life (*Peirush HaGra L'Safra D'Tzniusa*).

Of course, the somewhat lengthy descriptions of the Mishkan (Tabernacle) and the Priestly Garments likewise contain this aspect, wherein the loftiest and most cherished Torah secrets lay within the sacred words. In a more general sense, R' Chaim Shmuelevitz (*Sichos Mussar, vol. I, §9*) provides us with at least a fractional glimpse of some of the exalted substance reflected in the Mishkan-related *parshiyos*. At the same time, his words serve as a poignant reminder – and a good summary – of what this section is all about.

The Medrash presents a parable, illustrating the "dilemma" that gave rise to the idea of a Mishkan: The king's only daughter was betrothed to a prince from another land, who wished to return to his kingdom following the marriage. The king related his quandary to the newlywed couple: "I cannot part with my beloved daughter; on the other hand, she is now your wife, and I cannot withhold her from you. So I ask of you this one favor: Take her and go in peace, but please – build a private room for me by your dwelling, so that I may stay by the side of my only daughter." This is what the Almighty told Yisrael: "I have given you My beloved Torah. I cannot part from Her, but I cannot either withhold Her from you. Build Me a Sanctuary wherein My Presence can reside, so that I may remain with My beloved Torah" (*Shemos Rabbah 33:1*).

This is the essence of the Mishkan – Hashem's "abode" here on earth. Chazal tell us further that "For whatever Hashem created in the Upper Realms, He created a corresponding entity in the Lower World (of somewhat constricted quality to conform with the limitations of this world)" (*ibid., 33:4*). The Medrash lists some examples, such as the cherubic figures adorning the Holy Ark, which correspond to the angelic Cherubs that minister in Hashem's Court.

A wondrous reality emerges from these teachings of Chazal. The numerous details spelled out in this week's and previous *parshiyos* certainly do not represent a haphazard and redundant dissertation. Rather, this is a blueprint of the Abode of the Almighty Himself.

לזכר ולעילוי נשמות
חיים בן יוסף ע"ה
איטא טילי בת שמואל יעקב ע"ה

SEFER VAYIKRA

ספר ויקרא

לזכר ולעילוי נשמות

יעקב בן שלמה ע"ה
פראזל בת ר' יעקב אליה ע"ה

מנדל יוסף בן יצחק ע"ה
גיטל בת אלחנן ע"ה

VAYIKRA

The "Kuntz" of Being Humble

THERE IS A WELL-KNOWN ANECDOTE RELATED about a particular *Yamim Nora'im* (High Holy Days) experience. At one point in the service, the rabbi was apparently overcome with the emotion of the moment. He suddenly cast himself upon the floor, declaring: "*Oy*, Ribbono Shel Olam (Master of the Universe), *ich bin a gornisht* (I am a nothing)!"

The *shul's* president, seated nearby in his place of honor, soon followed suit. Falling to the ground, he likewise remarked: "*Oy*, Ribbono Shel Olam, *ich bin a gornisht!*"

That year, the officiating *chazan* (cantor) was new; imported from abroad, he was performing in this congregation for the first time. Witnessing this spectacle, he decided to adopt the practice. Bowing on the floor, he exclaimed as well, "Ribbono Shel Olam, *ich bin a gornisht!*"

But when the first two veterans beheld the *chazan's* entreaty, they were aghast. With a look of disdain, the president said, "Who does he think he is, that he calls himself a *gornisht!*"

KINDLY TAKE A MOMENT TO STUDY MISHNAS CHAYIM IN THE MERIT OF
ROCHEL BAS GEDALYAH A"H
A FELLOW JEW WHO PASSED AWAY WITH NO RELATIVES TO ARRANGE TORAH STUDY ON BEHALF OF HER *NESHAMAH*

While a fabrication, this incident actually contains a pertinent lesson. As we shall see, it could be that the president's words contain a kernel of truth.

Selective Modesty?

A STRIKING FEATURE OF THE FIRST WORD OF *SEFER* Vayikra is the fact that the letter *alef* in "Vayikra" is written in the Torah in miniature form (appearing something like this: ויקרא). The Ba'al Haturim explains the significance. In communicating with Moshe, Hashem employed the term ויקרא – He called, which demonstrates closeness and affection. This stands in contrast to the way Hashem communicated with the wicked Bilam, employing the shortened term of ויקר, implying a mere chance encounter and conveying a sense of disapproval and aloofness. Moshe, taking dictation from Hashem in writing the entire Torah, was told to write the full term ויקרא at the beginning of this week's *parshah*, indicating Hashem's regard for him. In his humility, however, Moshe did not want to attribute such stature to himself. And so, as if trying to substitute the less praiseworthy version of ויקר, he minimized the final letter, the *alef*, of ויקרא.

One of the remarkable aspects of this display of humility – the commentators point out – is that in a different instance Moshe apparently acquiesced to using this term. This is not the first time the term ויקרא appears in connection with Hashem's speaking with Moshe. Way back in *parshas* Yisro, as the Revelation at Sinai was just getting underway, the *passuk* states: וַיֵּרֶד ד' עַל־הַר סִינַי... וַיִּקְרָא ד' לְמֹשֶׁה אֶל־רֹאשׁ הָהָר – "And Hashem descended upon Har Sinai... and Hashem called to Moshe to the top of the mountain" (*Shemos* 19:20). There, the word is spelled out in full, with no letters reduced in size. If Moshe was uncomfortable with this term on account of his humility, why did he allow it to "go through" in this instance? Why did he wait until *parshas* Vayikra to try to deflect the glory from himself?

The Virtues of... Fame and Fortune

THERE IS A STATEMENT OF CHAZAL THAT DELIVERS what may appear to be a surprising message. Understanding the intent, however, can help clarify the issue above. Speaking of the qualifications for prophecy, the Gemara states (*Nedarim 38a*): אֵין הקב״ה מַשְׁרֶה שְׁכִינָתוֹ אֶלָּא עַל גִּבּוֹר וְעָשִׁיר וְחָכָם וְעָנָיו – "Hashem only rests His Presence on (someone who is) mighty, wealthy, sagacious and humble." The latter two characteristics – wisdom and humility – seem to be appropriate prerequisites for high spiritual achievement. But how are we to understand that might and wealth are considered desirable and necessary for the attainment of prophetic vision?

To be sure, the Rambam (*Shemoneh Perakim*) understands that Chazal were not referring here to physical strength and material wealth; rather, the qualities under discussion are those that reflect true and inherent might and wealth, as described in the familiar Mishnah in Avos (*4:1*):

אֵיזֶהוּ גִבּוֹר הַכּוֹבֵשׁ אֶת יִצְרוֹ... אֵיזֶהוּ עָשִׁיר הַשָּׂמֵחַ בְּחֶלְקוֹ...

"Who is (truly) mighty? One who subdues his evil inclination... Who is wealthy? One who is happy with his lot..."

However, R' Chaim Volozhiner provides a way of understanding the above teaching of Chazal even in the literal sense; that is, yes – the physical attributes of strength and monetary wealth are prerequisites for attaining prophecy! How could this be? R' Chaim explains that, in truth, the primary quality that makes a person suited for this spiritual attainment is the trait of *anivus*, true humility. *And it is specifically for this reason that one must first attain success in the material realm before achieving prophecy.* How can it be determined that one is truly humble? A person in difficult and debilitating circumstances might simply be reacting in the most natural way to his situation. In other words, it may not be such a colossal accomplishment for a pauper to refrain from feelings of haughtiness. The real test is when a person is "on top of the world" (or at least what the superficial multitudes consider to be the epitome of success). When a person is blessed with tremendous wealth and abilities – and can nevertheless cultivate a sense of earnest humility – *that* is truly a "*kuntz*" ("trick"). And that is true humility. Indeed, it is when a person rises to a position of grandeur that he deserves credit for (honestly) considering himself a mere "*gornisht.*" Such a person, then, is ready to receive the Divine Spirit.

The Gemara that lists these qualifications for attaining prophecy derived them from the example of Moshe Rabbeinu. From where do we see that he was wealthy? The Gemara learns this from Hashem's instruction to Moshe to carve the second tablets that would contain the Aseres Hadibros (Ten Commandments) – "*Pesal lecha* – You shall carve for you" (*Shemos* 34:1). This implies that he would be able to keep the remaining pieces of stone, which were extremely valuable (*cf. also Rashi, ibid.*).

Thus we see that Moshe Rabbeinu became wealthy *after* the episode of the breaking of the original tablets, well after the Revelation at Sinai. This explains why he "waited" until this week's *parshah* (which occurred even later) to minimize the *alef*. The "Vayikra" term appeared initially in *parshas* Yisro, describing events that took place *before* the giving of the Torah – when Moshe had not yet become wealthy. As such, he hadn't yet "earned the right" to "call himself a *gornisht.*" Only once he had attained wealth was a display of humility truly meaningful; and so it was here in *parshas* Vayikra that he first used the small *alef* (*Peninim Mishulchan Gavohah*).

לזכר ולעילוי נשמת

אהרן ע"ה בן ישעיה הלוי נ"י

TZAV

Relating to Children – at the Seder

A halachic *analysis of the parameters of the seasonal obligation to relate the Exodus narrative to one's children.*

AS IS WELL KNOWN, PRACTICED AND APPRECIATED, the Seder night is characterized as a remarkable educational opportunity, a time of profound interaction as one generation relates to the next, in many senses of the word. Not only are we enjoined to discuss the narrative of Yetziyas Mitzrayim (leaving Egypt), but there is a specific mitzvah to relate these events to one's children. As the *passuk* states (*Shemos 13:8*): וְהִגַּדְתָּ לְבִנְךָ בַּיּוֹם הַהוּא לֵאמֹר בַּעֲבוּר זֶה עָשָׂה ד' לִי בְּצֵאתִי מִמִּצְרָיִם – "And you shall tell your son on that day, saying: 'Because of this, Hashem did for me as I left Mitzrayim.'"

KINDLY TAKE A MOMENT TO STUDY MISHNAS CHAYIM IN THE MERIT OF
SOROH LEAH BAS MATISYOHU A"H
A FELLOW JEW WHO PASSED AWAY WITH NO RELATIVES TO ARRANGE TORAH STUDY ON BEHALF OF HER *NESHAMAH*

R' DAVID SOLOVEITCHIK (*ME'OREI HAMO'ADIM*, *Pesach*) addresses the following question, entailing a scenario that

International Complications is not uncommon these days. A certain individual who lived abroad was visiting his children who lived in Eretz Yisrael. The Seder of the first night presented no problems, of course; it was the second night when things became interesting. This man's children were permanent residents of the Land; as such, they observed only one day of *yom tov* and hence needed to attend only one Seder. The father, a resident of the diaspora and visiting only temporarily in Eretz Yisrael, had two Sedarim to attend: one the first night and one the second.

This is where the issue arose: On the second night, the visiting father had to conduct a Seder; his children did not. What was he supposed to do vis-a-vis the obligation of "*v'higadeta l'vincha* – you shall relate to your children"? Is this considered *his* obligation, such that he would have to bring his sons into the picture – despite the fact that for them, it was *chol hamo'ed* (intermediate festival days), and they had no formal Seder obligations? Or is the general obligation considered one that rests upon the children, i.e., *they* need to receive instruction from their father on this night? If that were the case, the "*v'higadeta l'vincha*" obligation would not be applicable here.

Basically, the question boils down to the following: Children, no doubt, are the most precious commodity of the Jewish people, the symbol of our continued existence and our future. When considering the overall mitzvah of "*v'higadeta l'vincha,*" however, we must analyze what technical, legalistic role they play in the mitzvah. Is it chiefly their obligation, such that, so to speak, it is up to them to solicit their father's telling of the story? If that is the case, then in our scenario, their presence at their father's second-night Seder is not necessary. Since the primary obligation is theirs anyway, tonight they have no obligation; they're off the hook and can go their merry way.

But the obligation could be understood from a completely different perspective, one that emanates chiefly from the father's standpoint. Take, for example, the mitzvah of the four *minim* (species) that are taken on Sukkos. That is an obligation that falls squarely on the individual, in which he uses a specific *cheftzah shel mitzvah* (mitzvah item) – in this case a *lulav* and *esrog* – to fulfill his personal obligation. Perhaps it is the same with regard to the Passover obligation of *"v'higadeta l'vincha."* In other words, it is chiefly the father's personal obligation to relate the story of Yetziyas Mitzrayim; from a technical standpoint, his children in this case are no more than a *"cheftzah shel mitzah,"* his *lulav* and *esrog* with which he will fulfill his obligation. This is no mere intellectual hypothesizing but carries bona-fide ramifications: in the case of our overseas visitor, he would need to enlist his "Israeli" children if this were the case. Their personal obligation is actually irrelevant; for purposes of this mitzvah, they are his *lulav* and *esrog*. He needs children of his own present at his Seder in order to fulfill *his* obligation of relating the story to his children.

Off the Hook

R' DAVID RULES LENIENTLY IN THIS CASE. HE BASES his reasoning on a Talmudic passage stemming from the following Mishnah in Kiddushin (1:7):

כָּל מִצְוֹת הַבֵּן עַל הָאָב, אֲנָשִׁים חַיָּבִין וְנָשִׁים פְּטוּרוֹת.

"(The general rule is:) Any mitzvah involving one's child, the obligation of which is incumbent on the parent – men are required to perform, while women are exempt."

In other words, there are certain *mitzvos* that a parent must perform on behalf of his child. In such instances, it is the father's (not mother's) obligation to see that the deed is discharged.

What are these *mitzvos*? The Gemara (*Kiddushin 29a*) lists a number of examples: *milah* (circumcision), *pidyon haben* (redemption of the first-born), Torah education, etc.

Conspicuously missing from the list, however, is what one would have assumed to be the quintessential "*mitzvas haben al ha'av*" – the mitzvah of "*v'higadeta l'vincha,*" – you shall relate to your child (about the Exodus).

Why, indeed, was this item omitted from the list? R' David concludes that, apparently, this mitzvah is *not* one that is imposed on the father; rather, it is *the children's own obligation* to solicit their father's instruction.

In that case, then, they are indeed not considered simply the father's *lulav* and *esrog,* means through which he carries out his personal obligation. Rather, they themselves carry their own obligation. Since the emphasis is placed on them, we examine their status of obligation. As such, in our scenario (residents of the Land on the second night of Pesach in Eretz Yisrael), they need not be in attendance at the Seder.

There is another ramification to this general question regarding the mitzvah of "*v'higadeta l'vincha*": In a regular case (all family members reside in the same country, and share the Passover obligations on the same day), need one relate (the story) to *all* of one's children? R' David points out that this would seem to depend, once again, on the two possibilities discussed above. If we assume that it is primarily a mitzvah incumbent on the children, then they would *each* need to be told, for each of them has his own obligation. However, if it is the father's obligation, and they are just "mitzvah objects," the means through which he discharges his obligation, it would be an entirely different story. If this is the case, by even relating the story to one child – lo and behold, the father's obligation has been discharged.

לזכר ולעילוי נשמת
ARNOLD BEN REUVAIN A"H

SHEMINI

Silence – Not Always Golden

UNDERSTANDING THE EVENTS IN THIS WEEK'S *parshah* that occurred with Nadav and Avihu, the two sons of Aharon Hakohein, is no simple matter. They did "something" and were burned to death (*Vayikra 10:2*). We are reminded, however, that these were individuals of tremendous spiritual stature. Remarking to his brother, Moshe Rabbeinu asserts that "they were greater than me and you" (*Rashi, ibid. v. 3*). There is much discussion concerning the exact nature of the misdeed that caused their demise. Whatever it was, the Medrash states further that this was the *only* sin they had ever committed (*Vayikra Rabbah 20:8*).

As such, it is important to bear in mind that this was no "ordinary" sin committed by "ordinary" people. As individuals of such pristine and elevated levels, it can only be understood as a very miniscule deed, one considered a flaw only for people whose greatness had reached such heights.

KINDLY TAKE A MOMENT TO STUDY MISHNAS CHAYIM IN THE MERIT OF
RAIZEL BAS FEIVEL HAKOHEN A"H
A FELLOW JEW WHO PASSED AWAY WITH NO RELATIVES TO ARRANGE TORAH STUDY ON BEHALF OF HER *NESHAMAH*

Biding Their Time?

SOME IDEA AS TO THE NATURE OF THE OFFENSE CAN be gleaned from the following Talmudic passage. It records a conversation that took place between the two brothers. At first glance, however, the sentiments they expressed don't seem to be on par with their supremely refined characters. The Gemara relates the following exchange that occurred in the midst of a procession: וּכְבָר הָיוּ מֹשֶׁה וְאַהֲרֹן מְהַלְּכִין בַּדֶּרֶךְ וְנָדָב וַאֲבִיהוּא מְהַלְּכִין אַחֲרֵיהֶן וְכָל יִשְׂרָאֵל אַחֲרֵיהֶן. אָמַר לוֹ נָדָב לַאֲבִיהוּא: אֵימָתַי יָמוּתוּ שְׁנֵי זְקֵנִים הַלָּלוּ וַאֲנִי וְאַתָּה נַנְהִיג אֶת הַדוֹר? אָמַר לָהֶן הַקָּדוֹשׁ בָּרוּךְ הוּא: הַנִּרְאֶה מִי קוֹבֵר אֶת מִי. "Moshe and Aharon were walking along the way, Nadav and Avihu walked behind them and all Yisrael behind them. Nadav said to Avihu: 'When will these two elders die, and I and you will lead the generation?' Hashem said to them: 'Let us see who will bury whom'" (Sanhedrin 52a).

This certainly does not seem like the kind of talk one would expect from otherwise perfect *tzaddikim* (righteous men) who had never sinned in their lives! How could it be that they even harbored such seemingly callous and self-centered sentiments, let alone actually spoke with such apparent contempt about the righteous leaders Aharon (their father!) and Moshe?

It should be noted – as the Chida does (*Pesach Einayim, Sanhedrin ibid.*) – that, in truth, only one of the brothers did the *actual* speaking: "*Nadav said* to Avihu: 'When will...'" In fact, this point helps to clarify another perplexing issue. The *passuk* in Iyov (*37:1*) states: לְזֹאת יֶחֱרַד לִבִּי – "At this, my heart trembled." The Medrash (*cf. Tanchuma, Parshas Acharei Mos*) identifies the event that occasioned this comment as the death of Aharon's two sons.

Why was Iyov so distraught over this occurrence? The Chida explains that it stemmed from his previous occupation as an advisor to Pharaoh. Chazal tell us (*Sotah 11a*) that it was Iyov's colleague Bilam who suggested that B'nei Yisrael be enslaved; Iyov remained silent. He thought that in this way he would escape punishment for conspiring against Hashem's people.

And so, when later learning of Nadav and Avihu's demise, Iyov was terrified. They had been taken to task for the unbefitting comments about Moshe and Aharon. But it was actually only Nadav who made the remarks – Avihu had merely listened! From the fact that *both* were punished, Iyov concluded that one is held accountable for keeping silent when the situation calls for protest. He feared and regretted his own silence regarding the plan against the Jews.

Laudable Intentions

IT EMERGES, THEN, THAT THE ACTUAL "PERPETRATOR" was only one of the brothers. But this brother as well, as we have seen, was of an extremely elevated spiritual stature. These comments seem totally incongruous with his level, as well as that of his righteous brother, who seems to have been complicit in the sentiment. What could they have been thinking?

The commentators offer some eye-opening solutions, demonstrating that, of course, the brothers were the farthest thing from crass glory-seekers. The venerated R' Ephraim Zalman Margolis (known as the Beis Ephraim) explains their expressed yearning – headed by the term *"masai"* (when) – in line with another well-known phrase beginning in the same way. The Medrash (*Tanna D'vei Eliyahu Rabbah 23:1*) encourages every Jew to declare: מָתַי יַגִּיעוּ מַעֲשַׂי לְמַעֲשֵׂי אַבְרָהָם יִצְחָק וְיַעֲקֹב? "When will my deeds reach those of Avraham, Yitzchak, and Ya'akov?" Such a declaration reveals an inner desire to grow spiritually and attain ever-greater closeness to the Almighty. This was the nature of the brothers' comments, as well. In stating אֵימָתַי יָמוּתוּ שְׁנֵי זְקֵנִים הַלָּלוּ וַאֲנִי וְאַתָּה נַנְהִיג אֶת הַדּוֹר?, they were not eagerly anticipating the death of these two luminaries. Rather, they were expressing their esteem for Moshe and Aharon, reflecting the sentiment of the Tanna D'vei Eliyahu: "When," they wondered aloud, "will our deeds approach theirs, such that we would even be worthy of succeeding their august leadership?" (*K'motzei Shalal Rav, Vayikra 10:2*).

Another possibility is that, rather than eager anticipation, Nadav and Avihu were actually expressing a sense of dread. Their sentiment was actually in keeping with the following brief but profound teaching from the Mishnah in Avos (*1:10*):

שְׁמַעְיָה אוֹמֵר... שְׂנָא אֶת הָרַבָּנוּת.

> "Shemayah says... (One should) despise (the prospect of holding) a position of authority."

R' Yitzchak Aharon Rappaport, Maggid of Wilkomir thus explains the brothers' statement as emanating from worry. They knew that assuming the mantle of leadership would result in a severe curtailment of their own Torah studies and spiritual pursuits. As such, Moshe and Aharon's advancing age was a source of real concern to them (*K'motzei Shalal Rav, ibid.*).

Thus, their conversation speaks more of their elevated nature than of character blemish. Because of their great piety, they were held to extremely high standards, made responsible perhaps more for the appearance of impropriety than any inherent, deep flaw. And through them was fulfilled the dictum "Through those close to Me, I become sanctified" (*Vayikra 10:3*).

לזכר ולעילוי נשמת
פרומא לאה בת אברהם ושמחה ע"ה

TAZRIA-METZORA

Bringing Down the House

An exhibition on the underpinnings of the topic of tzara'as habayis *(type of surface disease, here affecting a house).*

THE COMMENTATORS REVEAL THE WEALTH OF profundity contained within the details of the *tzara'as* chapter, the main subject of this double *parshah*. Here, we attempt to at least scratch the surface regarding one of these aspects, the phenomenon of *tzara'as habayis* (*Vayikra 14:33-53*). As we shall see, there are various facets to this occurrence – some well-known, others less so.

CHAZAL INFORM US (*PRIMARILY IN ARACHIN* [16A]) that (general) *tzara'as* results from any number of specific flaws or misdeeds. However, it is quite a unique form of punishment. Perhaps more than any other type of retribution, *tzara'as* is characterized by *bushah* (embarrassment), as the afflicted sinner suffers great shame in the course of his ordeal. Among other practices, he must

Tzara'as is Embarassing

KINDLY TAKE A MOMENT TO STUDY MISHNAS CHAYIM IN THE MERIT OF
FAIGEL BAS SHMUEL A"H
A FELLOW JEW WHO PASSED AWAY WITH NO RELATIVES TO ARRANGE TORAH STUDY ON BEHALF OF HER *NESHAMAH*

rend his clothes, sit by himself and publicly announce his state of defilement (*Vayikra 13:45-46*).

The Chafetz Chaim (*Shemiras Halashon, II, ch. 16*) highlights another practice through which the "embarrassment factor" is quite apparent. When someone would bring a sacrifice in Temple times, it was accompanied by a libation offering (which differed in such particulars as quantity, based on the type of sacrifice it was accompanying). The Mishnah (*Shekalim 5:3*) outlines the interesting procedure through which these libations were procured. The individual bringing the sacrifice would have to purchase whatever he needed for the libation offering from the Temple officers. He would first approach one officer, tell him what kind of sacrifice he was bringing and transfer the necessary funds to him. Having calculated the nature of the mandated libation offering, the officer would then hand this customer a ticket of sorts (a *chosem* – seal), upon which was inscribed a term signifying the designated libation. As the Mishnah states:

אַרְבָּעָה חוֹתָמוֹת הָיוּ בַּמִּקְדָּשׁ, וְכָתוּב עֲלֵיהֶן, עֵגֶל, זָכָר, גְּדִי, חוֹטֵא... חוֹטֵא מְשַׁמֵּשׁ עִם... מְצוֹרָעִין.

"*There were four (types of) seals utilized in the Temple. Upon them were written (one of the following terms): 'Calf,' 'ram,' 'kid,' or 'sinner'... The one (upon which was written) 'sinner' was used in connection with ... the (purification procedure of) those afflicted with tzara'as.*"

Thus branded in so explicit a manner, the afflicted man would have to present his ticket to the libation officer to receive his libation materials. The humiliation he had to endure was intended to make him contrite and effect an atonement for the sins that had brought him to this state.

Shame plays a significant role, as well, in the procedure for dealing with *tzara's habayis*. Chazal attribute such *tzara'as* as being caused by the flaw of *tzarus ayin* (stinginess and selfishness). Based on the Medrash (*Vayikra Rabbah 17:2*), the *Tzror Hamor* (*parshas*

Metzora) illustrates what transpires: Neighbors would come to borrow this or that household item. Unfortunately, this particular householder never learned to share. Whenever he was asked, "Could I use your shovel?" "Could I borrow your sifter?" he would say, "I'm sorry, but I don't own one."

As outlined in the Torah, a house inflicted with *tzara'as* needed to be seen by the *kohein*. Before he would conduct his examination and pronounce the house to be in a state of defilement, the owner was to remove all of his possessions from the house (so as to prevent them from contracting defilement as well). Clearing everything out from one's house is no simple matter, and so, the owner would have to enlist his neighbors to assist in the job. Everyone was gathered round and handling his objects; lo and behold, they would suddenly come upon the shovel and sifter he supposedly didn't own! In front of the whole neighborhood, his stinginess was laid bare.

Demonic Disease

RASHI (*VAYIKRA 14:34*), BASED ON THE MEDRASH, cites the benevolent feature of *tzara'as habayis*: namely, that it served as a tremendous financial windfall for the homeowner. This was due to the fact that the Emori, original inhabitants of Eretz Yisrael, had stored treasures within the walls of their houses in anticipation of B'nei Yisrael's imminent invasion. With the onset of *tzara'as* and by following the procedure of examination and dismantling as outlined in the *parshah*, the owner would discover that the walls of his structure were laden with gold.

Elsewhere, Chazal reveal that the Emori had used quite unusual "building materials" in fashioning their houses. Apparently, there was a lot more in those walls than hidden treasure.

Based on the Zohar, the *Tzror Hamor* (*parshas Metzora*) imparts the remarkable fact that the Emori's houses were actually established on a foundation that was spiritual in nature – and not necessarily from the good side. These people were notorious for being steeped in idolatrous practices and the use of magic, drawing on the impure spiritual forces. Thus, they would lay the cornerstone of their house in the name of this or that *sheid* (demon), thereby infusing their house with a force of impurity that would permeate their dwelling and their lives. When Klal Yisrael entered the Land, Hashem did not want His holy nation to reside in a Land and in dwellings which were essentially contaminated (in a dark, spiritual sense). He would thus cause these "house demons" (referred to in kabbalistic literature as "*ba'alei batim*") to expand and emerge from the inner recesses – appearing and spreading in the form of *tzara'as habayis*. This would result in a visit by the *kohein*, a man of sanctified status, who would begin the process to ultimately eradicate and "exorcise" the impure forces from the lives of the Jewish inhabitants.

The *Tzror Hamor* explains some of the details of the procedure based on this idea. For example, when the *kohein* would confer official impure status on the house, it would then be closed off for a period of seven days. The *Tzror Hamor* reveals the basis for this specific time period: it was to ensure that a Shabbos will transpire in the interim. This was a crucial event, for Shabbos proves detrimental to the *sheidim*. The Mishnah in Avos (5:6) mentions that demons were created during the week of Creation, in the period of "*bein hashemashos*" on *erev* Shabbos, meaning that they were formed in the final moments before the onset of the first Shabbos. This indicates that they are inherently incomplete creatures – disembodied souls, for the most part – whereby Shabbos arrived, and in a sense, interrupted their creation before they were fully formed. This left them in a state of terror vis-à-vis Shabbos, always attempting to flee from its arrival. So, in trying to evict these unwanted residents from the houses of Eretz Yisrael, Shabbos was enlisted to chase them away, restoring each residence to a pristine state.

לזכר ולעילוי נשמות
הרב משה דוד בן הרב אברהם יצחק זצ״ל
רבקה בת הרב צבי ע״ה

ACHAREI MOS-KEDOSHIM

The Logic behind Wonders

A SENIOR *TALMID CHACHAM* (TORAH SCHOLAR) from the previous generation related the following about the Baba Sali, the venerated Sephardic Kabbalistic figure:

THE BABA SALI, SAINTLY AND MUCH REMOVED FROM the materialistic plane, was once en route to a certain function. The vehicle that was transporting him started experiencing some trouble and eventually broke down. Turning to the driver, the Baba Sali asked what the problem was. Of course, the technical explanation of the mechanical failure didn't mean much to him.

Start Your Engines

So the Baba Sali tried a different tack: "Could you show me where the issue lies?" he queried. Shrugging his shoulders, the driver pointed at one of the mechanical features of the car. The sage then removed his handkerchief, recited a Kabbalistic formula and

---

KINDLY TAKE A MOMENT TO STUDY MISHNAS CHAYIM IN THE MERIT OF
CHAYAH BAS SHMUEL A"H
A FELLOW JEW WHO PASSED AWAY WITH NO RELATIVES TO ARRANGE TORAH STUDY ON BEHALF OF HER *NESHAMAH*

pressed the handkerchief to that part of the vehicle. The car revved up, and they were back on their way.

Needless to say, even if we were somehow privy to whatever formula the Baba Sali used, this method probably wouldn't work if you or I tried it. When we hear accounts like this, we may be left feeling somewhat wistful, marveling at the "power" of some of these angelic figures.

Without any intent, G-d forbid, to minimize the stature of those individuals who are truly great, the truth of the matter is that such instances may not necessarily be such a "wonder." Consider, for example, Chazal's remarkable description regarding those who attain the exalted level of learning Torah *lishmah* (for its own sake). As the Mishnah states (*Avos 6:2*):

> רַבִּי מֵאִיר אוֹמֵר כָּל הָעוֹסֵק בַּתּוֹרָה לִשְׁמָהּ, זוֹכֶה לִדְבָרִים הַרְבֵּה. וְלֹא עוֹד אֶלָּא שֶׁכָּל הָעוֹלָם כֻּלּוֹ כְּדַאי הוּא לוֹ... וּמְגַדַּלְתּוֹ וּמְרוֹמַמְתּוֹ עַל כָּל הַמַּעֲשִׂים.

> *"R' Meir says: Whoever engages in Torah study for its own sake merits many things. Furthermore, the (creation of) the entire world was worthwhile for his sake alone... And it causes him to become greater and uplifted over 'all of the works.'"*

The *Medrash Shmuel* elucidates the meaning of this curious phrase – "uplifted over 'all of the works.'" He explains it as referring to the works of Creation; that is, this exalted individual gains mastery over the entirety of Creation – "all of its works," including even the *malachim* (angels). He states further that one who attains the level of which the Mishnah speaks is literally able to do anything he wants and put any plan into action. "Even if he would want to create under the sun that which was not created during the six days of Creation," the *Medrash Shmuel* asserts, "he would be able to do so."

T O A LARGE EXTENT, THIS ABILITY WAS GRANTED to Klal Yisrael at the time of the giving of the Torah at Har Sinai.

The Rules of Nature Were Meant to be Broken

The Gemara (*Berachos 5a*) contrasts Hashem's giving of the Torah with a seller whose pressing financial circumstances force him to part with one of his beloved possessions: "Come and see how Hashem's attitude differs from that of people... When a person must sell his possession to his fellow, the seller is saddened, and only the buyer is happy. Hashem conducts Himself differently; He remained joyful even as He gave the Torah to Yisrael, as it states (*Mishlei 4:2*), 'For I have given you a good purchase; do not abandon My Torah.'"

R' Elazar Moshe Horowitz (*commentary to Berachos*) wonders about the comparison. Aren't the two instances completely dissimilar? In the case of the desperate seller, he was sad because he had to part with his favored object. How does this apply in the case of Hashem's giving of the Torah? When someone teaches Torah to another, does the teacher "lose" the Torah? Certainly not; he simply imparts and shares his knowledge with his students. How could the Gemara imply that there was equivalency in the case of Hashem's granting the Torah to Yisrael?

R' Elazar Moshe clarifies the Gemara's intent along the lines discussed above. Yes, he explains, in a sense, Hashem did "lose" something by giving the Torah to Yisrael. He lost exclusive dominance over Creation. Previously, this was His domain alone. With the giving of the Torah, however, Klal Yisrael also gained the ability to wield influence and control over Creation.

The notion that, through Torah, a Yid gains "supernatural" ability is manifest in our *parshah*. *Parshas* Kedoshim, of course, opens with the theme of *kedushah* (sanctity): קְדֹשִׁים תִּהְיוּ כִּי קָדוֹשׁ אֲנִי ד' אֱלֹקֵיכֶם – "Be holy, for I, Hashem your G-d, am holy" (*Vayikra 19:2*). The *passuk* seems to link Yisrael's need for sanctity with the fact that Hashem is holy, as the Sifra to this verse expounds: "If you make yourselves holy, I will consider it to you as if you made Me holy. If you do not make yourselves holy, I will consider it to you as if you did not make Me holy." The Sifra's rendering seems difficult to understand. What does it even mean to "make Hashem holy"? And what is this interrelationship implied by the Sifra?

The Malbim explains that herein is contained a very fundamental principle regarding the workings of the world. There are, in fact, two types of "*hanhagos*" – two ways in which Hashem conducts the communal and individual affairs of men. One is the "*hanhagas hateva*," the conduct of the world through the "natural" order. The other way in which Hashem runs the world is through the "*hanhagah nisis*" – miraculous conduct, which transcends the laws of nature.

What determines which "*hanhagah*" Hashem will employ? This, explains the Malbim, is dependent on Yisrael themselves. And this is what the Sifra means by "sanctifying Hashem," even though He is already the epitome and essence of sanctity. What is "sanctity" as it applies to a person? A mode of conduct in which a person elevates himself against and above his natural inclinations. If a person chooses to remain subservient to his innate desires, allowing his "nature" to dictate his path in life – Hashem will follow suit. He will also conduct affairs according to the "natural order" of things. This arrangement, history shows, does not always work out so well for the Jewish people, as the nations of the world are naturally aligned against the Jews and yearn and strive for their destruction. But if a person fights against and subdues his "*teva*," then Hashem will respond in kind. He will also be "sanctified," entailing a transfer from the *hanhagas hateva* to the *hanhagah nisis*.

Our *parshah*, then, contains the key to miracles – which is also the key to the existence of the Jewish people. This key is *kedushah*: transcending one's nature. The results can be wondrous.

לזכר ולעילוי נשמות
אהרן יהושע בן מאיר אריה ע"ה
אסתר בת זאב ע"ה

EMOR

Praying for Rain

AMONG THE VARIOUS *MO'ADIM* (FESTIVALS) DEALT with in this week's *parshah* – each unique in its own way – is the *yom tov of* Shemini Atzeres. A superficial glance seems to suggest that there is not much "happening" on this *yom tov*, especially in contrast to the entire Sukkos festival that preceded it. Sukkos was categorized by visible mitzvah fulfillment in abundance, in the form of *sukkah, lulav* and *esrog* and the many practices observed throughout the festival. For all intents and purposes, these all come to an end with the advent of Shemini Atzeres. This glaring contrast is manifest as well with regard to the Temple service. The sacrificial order throughout Sukkos itself is quite elaborate, entailing a large number of animals. These include the great quantity of bulls that were offered, beginning with thirteen on the first day, twelve on the second, etc. By the end of the Sukkos festival, a total of seventy bulls had been offered, corresponding to the seventy nations of the world on whose behalf the sacrifices were intended. Yet, on Shemini Atzeres, the number of bulls offered is reduced to a single one.

KINDLY TAKE A MOMENT TO STUDY MISHNAS CHAYIM IN THE MERIT OF
RIVKAH BAS ELIEZER *A"H*
A FELLOW JEW WHO PASSED AWAY WITH NO RELATIVES TO ARRANGE TORAH STUDY ON BEHALF OF HER *NESHAMAH*

Chazal inform us that, in fact, this "pairing down" on Shemini Atzeres is actually a sign of Hashem's special love for and relationship with the Jewish people. As mentioned, the seventy bulls offered throughout Sukkos were intended to arouse favor for the nations of the world, that their welfare be sustained from on High. But the single bull offered on Shemini Atzeres is intended for the benefit of Klal Yisrael alone. By mandating this individualized sacrifice at this time, Hashem conveys the following sentiment to Yisrael: "Throughout this period, I have engaged in a great, communal celebration. Now, I desire a smaller, more intimate celebration with you alone" (*Sukkah 55b*).

A Matter of Practicality

THERE IS A CURIOUS PRACTICE WE FOLLOW AT THIS time, which is unique to the *yom tov* of Shemini Atzeres: Tefillas Geshem, the prayer for rain. This somewhat elaborate prayer is accorded great solemnity, offered in a manner reminiscent of the Yamim Nora'im (Days of Awe): the *chazzan* wears a *kittel*, and even the tune of the Yamim Nora'im *davening* is adopted for the occasion. Yet, the whole experience may appear somewhat mystifying: What occasions such an elaborate and "serious" ceremony? What is the connection specifically to Shemini Atzeres? It is true that we begin to insert into the Shemoneh Esrei the brief phrase of *mashiv haru'ach u'morid hageshem* ("He makes the wind blow and brings down the rain"). But what is the significance of such an extended version, characterized by such solemnity?

On the surface, it may be that practical considerations are at play here. As an essential for life, the need for rain is universally appreciated. "The world cannot exist without water," Chazal tell us (*Ta'anis 2b*). The world is judged for rain on Sukkos; the annual allotment is determined at this time (*Rosh Hashanah 16a*). A number of the Sukkos observances reflect an attempt to elicit a favorable judgment from Hashem on this matter. The four species, for example, are all heavily water-dependent, as is evident from how they are described in this week's *parshah*: "fruit of the tree that is *hadar* (identified by the Gemara as water-related)... willows of the river" (*Vayikra 23:40*). Nevertheless, we refrain from a full-blown petition for rain. R' Yehoshua explains that his reason for postponing the inclusion of *mashiv haru'ach* until the end of the festival is because rain during Sukkos can be detrimental. As stated in the Mishnah in Ta'anis (*1:1*):

רַבִּי יְהוֹשֻׁעַ אוֹמֵר... אֵין הַגְּשָׁמִים אֶלָּא סִימַן קְלָלָה בֶּחָג.

> "R' Yehoshua says: ...Rain during Sukkos is an inauspicious sign (revealing Hashem's displeasure with Yisrael's service, as rain preempts the mitzvah of staying in the sukkah)."

When Shemini Atzeres arrives – and the principal observance of *sukkah*-dwelling has ended – rain no longer constitutes a bad omen. As such, it is the first opportunity to render explicit and lengthy prayers for this life-giving element – which we do through the Tefillas Hageshem.

Rain from Heaven (Literally)

THE *SHEM MISHMUEL* (*SHEMINI ATZERES 5677*), however, offers an alternative and novel approach, revealing some of the depth inherent in this solemn rite. He bases his explanation on a Talmudic dispute that revolves around a central question: from where does rain originate?

"R' Eliezer says: The whole world derives its moisture from the ocean (i.e., through evaporation and other components of the rain-cycle)... R' Yehoshua says: The whole world derives its moisture from the '*mayim ha'elyonim*' (the upper waters)" (*Ta'anis 9a*).

The *mayim ha'elyonim* mentioned by R' Yehoshua refers to an item appearing in the Creation narrative of the second day: "And G-d made the firmament and separated between the waters that are below... and the waters that are above" (*Bereishis 1:7*). Identifying what these "upper waters" are is no simple matter; the Ramban contends that this verse represents a mystical concept, the true meaning of which lies beyond standard comprehension. At the very least, we can understand that it refers to something of an elevated, spiritual quality. Thus, the dispute between R' Eliezer and R' Yehoshua can be summed up as follows: does rain emanate from a *physical* source (R' Eliezer) or a *spiritual* one (R' Yehoshua)?

The *Shem Mishmuel* understands that, in fact, these two positions are not mutually exclusive, for rain actually contains *both* elements. What *we* see is the outer, sea-based "shell," which is its physical component. (The Hebrew term for rain – "**geshem**" – actually derives from the overall term for physicality –"**gashmiyus**" [*Rabbeinu Bechaye, Devarim 11:17*].) But it is apparently also imbued with an inner, *spiritual* essence, which stems from the ethereal "upper waters." (The Nesivos adds that those rains of exceptional beneficence known as "*gishmei berachah*" [rains of blessing] emanate specifically from the "upper waters" [*Nachalas Ya'akov, Ta'anis*].)

This dual arrangement is reflected in the nature of the festival. As mentioned, Sukkos is the time when the world is judged for rain; the seventy bull offerings, on behalf of the nations, have the effect of obtaining a favorable judgment for them. However, explains the *Shem Mishmuel*, their allotment is for the *physical* component of rain. But the loftier, more blessed and spiritual side of this Heavenly gift is reserved for the Jewish people alone.

This is the principal aim of the Tefillas Geshem. It is a unique prayer for singular, spiritual bounty, reflecting how special Klal Yisrael is to Hakadosh Baruch Hu. It is no coincidence, then, that it is offered on the very day that celebrates Hashem's special affinity for His people.

לזכר ולעילוי נשמות
יששכר דוב מרדכי בן אליעזר ע"ה
שרה לאה בת רפאל יוסף ע"ה

BEHAR-BECHUKOSAI

How Can You Sleep at Night?

THE PONEVEZHER RAV HAD A PROBLEM.

It was 1943, in the midst of the conflagration that was engulfing European Jewry. In his tireless efforts to secure some measure of rescue and relief for his imperiled brethren, the Ponevezher Rav had established Batei Avos in B'nei Brak, a refuge center for Jewish children escaping from the Holocaust. In a few days, the first group of young refugees would be arriving.

The problem was that the wartime disturbances were extremely far-reaching. In Eretz Yisrael itself many products were rationed or unavailable. It was simply impossible, even for all the money in the world, to procure sufficient bedding to accommodate the expected influx of refugees. Ravaged and exhausted from their flight, they were soon to arrive.

Finally, the Rav thought he had a plan. In an attempt to convey his idea to the *tzibbur* (community), he posed the following question in the context of a Shabbos address in *shul*.

KINDLY TAKE A MOMENT TO STUDY MISHNAS CHAYIM IN THE MERIT OF
KAYLA BAS YISROEL A"H
A FELLOW JEW WHO PASSED AWAY WITH NO RELATIVES TO ARRANGE TORAH STUDY ON BEHALF OF HER *NESHAMAH*

Who Comes First?

THE TORAH DISCUSSES THE INSTITUTION OF THE *eved Ivri*, a Jewish man who sells himself as a slave to another Jewish master. A number of laws apply to such a case, not the least of which is the firm obligation on the master to treat him with dignity and fairness. In fact, the Yerushalmi notes the extent to which the master must provide for this slave: He must supply him with a pillow, even if it is the only one he owns.

That means, of course, that the slave will go to sleep at night with a pillow, while the owner will not. While the self-sacrifice seems impressive, the Ponevezher Rav pointed out, it seems to contradict a different notion elsewhere.

The Gemara (*Bava Metzia 62a*) discusses a well-known and tragic case: Two people are wandering in the desert. One of them happens to have a flask of water with him; while there is enough to sustain him until he reaches civilization, the supply is insufficient to provide for both of them. The gut-wrenching question becomes: what to do? Do they share the water and suffer the identical fate? R' Akiva learns the proper course of action from this week's *parshah*. The *passuk* states (*Vayikra 25:36*): וְחֵי אָחִיךָ עִמָּךְ – "And your brother shall live with you." "With you," he shall live, but not instead. Thus, concludes R' Akiva: חַיֶּיךָ קוֹדְמִים לְחַיֵּי חֲבֵירְךָ – "Your life takes precedence over that of your friend."

This overriding principle is applicable to a number of situations. One should always try to provide assistance, of course. But if it's a mutually exclusive matter, one's own needs come first.

And so, asked the Ponevezher Rav, how are we to understand the *halachah* (rule) governing an *eved Ivri*? We learned that if the master has only one pillow, it goes to the slave. What happened to the *"chayecha kodmim"* principle? Shouldn't the master himself get the better night's sleep?

Good, Old-Fashioned "Jewish Guilt"

THE PONEVEZHER RAV PROCEEDED TO demonstrate how, even in this instance, the owner's needs are in fact given precedence. That is, the Torah realizes what will happen if the owner retains the pillow for himself – he won't be able to sleep! Knowing that he left his poor *eved* without a pillow would so gnaw at his conscience that he would toss and turn all night. By mandating that he give his one pillow to his slave, the master will be able to get a good night's sleep himself – pillow or no pillow!

"We, too, are in the same situation," the Ponevezher Rav told his audience. "In another day, the first wave of immigrants will be arriving. Alas, they have no pillows, and we have no way to acquire them. How will we be able to sleep at night, knowing that these poor orphans have no pillows? Unless, of course, we provide them with our own..."

Actually, it stands to reason that there was a lot more than just plain "guilt" that the Ponevezher Rav was banking on. Rather, he was aware of the inherent desire to do the right thing that lies deep within the hearts of every Jew – even the wanton sinner.

Consider the case discussed in the Mishnah (*Arachin* 5:6) of a recalcitrant husband who disobeys the order of the *beis din* (Jewish Court) to grant his wife a *get* (bill of divorce):

בְּגִטֵּי נָשִׁים, כּוֹפִין אוֹתוֹ עַד שֶׁיֹּאמַר רוֹצֶה אֲנִי.

> "With regard to bills of divorce, (beis din) can employ physical force to coerce (the man) into declaring: 'I consent (to the divorce).'"

One of the reasons this particular *halachah* is so remarkable is that a *get* is only valid if it is produced *with the husband's acquiescence*. And yet, such "acquiescence" is considered legitimate even if procured through the offices of thugs for hire.

How can this be? In a famous and fundamental dissertation, the Rambam (*Hilchos Geirushin 2:20*) explains that, in fact, even such an individual wishes to do right; it is merely his evil inclination that temporarily clouds his ability to think straight: "One whose evil inclination has taken hold of him, compelling him to neglect the fulfillment of a particular mitzvah or to commit a sin and is then beaten (by the authorities) until he performs that which he is obligated to do... this is not considered 'forced' (i.e., it is not truly 'against his will'); rather, it was he, himself, who had 'forced' himself to act improperly through his own corrupted mind. Therefore, regarding one who refuses (to adhere to the court's mandate that he divorce his wife), since inherently he wishes to be considered a member of Yisrael, *he truly wants to fulfill all of the mitzvos and refrain from all sins;* it is only that he has been overpowered by his inclination. However, once his inclination has been weakened and subdued through the beating he has sustained, and he pronounces, 'I acquiesce,' (this constitutes a manifestation of his true desire), and he has divorced with a full heart." In short, everyone inherently wants to do right, and will do so – if they can only get past the blockage of the *yetzer hara* (evil inclination).

לזכר ולעילוי נשמת
הרב שמעון בן הרב אברהם זצ"ל

SEFER BAMIDBAR

ספר במדבר

לזכר ולעילוי נשמות
שמשון מרדכי בן אהרן ע"ה
חיה בת יצחק ע"ה

BAMIDBAR

Grass and Torah

A Closer Look at a Time-Honored Shavuos Custom

UPON ENTERING THE SYNAGOGUE ON THE *YOM tov* of Shavuos, one is greeted by a most exhilarating sight – an array of greenery and/or other foliage. A similar type of adornment decorates the private residences of many Jews, as well.

Joy and Judgment

WHAT IS THE CENTRAL IDEA UPON WHICH THIS practice is based? The conventional understanding – which has the added benefit of being both true and documented – is that the greenery commemorates the vegetation surrounding Har Sinai at the time of the giving of the Torah. The Rema in Shulchan Aruch (*Orach Chaim 494:3*) records this view, stating: "It is our custom to spread grasses on Shavuos in the synagogue and the houses in remembrance of the joy of the giving of the Torah." The Mishnah Berurah (*ibid. §10*) clarifies that the Rema is referring to the aforementioned phenomenon – the greenery of the mountain.

The Mishnah Berurah elaborates there on an "offshoot" of this

---

KINDLY TAKE A MOMENT TO STUDY MISHNAS CHAYIM IN THE MERIT OF
AIDEL BAS YOEL A"H
A FELLOW JEW WHO PASSED AWAY WITH NO RELATIVES TO ARRANGE TORAH STUDY ON BEHALF OF HER *NESHAMAH*

custom: namely, setting out trees as decoration. This practice is based on the judgment factor mentioned in the Mishnah (*Rosh Hashanah* 1:3):

> בְּאַרְבָּעָה פְרָקִים הָעוֹלָם נִדּוֹן, בַּפֶּסַח עַל הַתְּבוּאָה, בָּעֲצֶרֶת עַל פֵּרוֹת הָאִילָן, בְּרֹאשׁ הַשָּׁנָה כָּל בָּאֵי הָעוֹלָם עוֹבְרִין לְפָנָיו... וּבֶחָג נִדּוֹנִין עַל הַמָּיִם.

> *"At four junctures throughout the year the world undergoes (a specific form of) judgment: On Pesach (the judgment is) for produce, on Shavuos for fruit of the tree, on Rosh Hashanah, all of humanity passes before Him (in judgment)... and on Sukkos, (the judgment is) for water."*

Thus, the placement of trees reflects the fact that this *yom tov* is a day of judgment for the fruit of the tree. However, as the Mishnah Berurah concludes, the Vilna Gaon abolished the particular practice of using trees for decoration once the gentiles engaged in a similar practice on their idolatrous holiday.

There exists yet another Shavuos custom relating to the earth's produce that is not as well known, but is mentioned in Chazal's work on Megillas Esther known as "Targum Sheni." Apparently drained from the troubles caused by their hostile gentile neighbors, the Jews would petition Hashem to remove them and their influence. They would express this sentiment in a most interesting way: On the *yom tov* of Shavuos, they would ascend to their rooftops and hurl down a cascade of apples, which they would then proceed to gather. In so doing, they would direct this prayer to Hashem: "Just as we gather these apples, so may You gather up our enemies from our midst."

Going Vegan

R' TZVI HIRSCH FROM OSTROW WAS A SAINTLY sage who devoted himself to Torah, completely unfazed by his abject poverty and the dilapidated conditions of his abode. He proffered a novel explanation of the custom of spreading greenery on Shavuos, as related in his name by R' Yitzchak Zilberstein (*Aleinu L'shabei'ach*,

Parshas Vayeilech). His approach is based on the Talmudic account of R' Ada bar Masna (*Eruvin 22a*). The Gemara was discussing the imperative to be willing, if necessary, to experience deprivation for the sake of Torah study – even to the extent that one's family might be affected. Of course, this does not mean that one can pain or torment them, *chas v'Shalom*. On the other hand, they might at times demand a certain standard of living whose maintenance would necessitate a mitigation of one's commitment to Torah. If that is the case, and there exists an alternative in consonance with the level of that particular generation, this could well be the preferred outcome.

And so the Gemara relates the example of R' Ada bar Masna who was to embark on an extended stay away from home, where he could engage in uninterrupted Torah study. Prior to his departure, his wife remarked: "With you away for such a long time, what will be with the children? Who will provide for them?" To which R' Ada responded: "There's plenty of grass in the field..."

As noted, this exact method may not be suitable for every generation – especially given the vast gap that exists between the spiritual levels of the former generations and the current one. But the message is eternal. As long as everyone is provided for – in a fashion deemed suitable for that particular situation – the needs of Torah should not be neglected. This, R' Tzvi Hirsh explains, is why we spread greenery on Shavuos. It reminds us at this opportune time, as we celebrate the giving of the Torah, what a commitment to Torah entails: it may very well require a substantial measure of *mesirus nefesh* – exertion and self-sacrifice. That is, one who desires to truly grow in Torah and develop into a *talmid chacham* (Torah scholar) must be willing to subject himself to "whatever it takes" to reach this goal, even to the point of subsisting on nothing but grass.

It is interesting to note that in recording this thought, R' Yitzchak Zilberstein was fulfilling the Talmudic dictum (*Chagigah 14a*) of נָאֶה דּוֹרֵשׁ וְנָאֶה מְקַיֵּים (the rough equivalent of which would be: "He practices what he preaches"); R' Yitzchak writes that he himself, at one point, had to endure conditions very similar to those experienced thousands of years earlier by the family of R' Ada bar Masna.

This took place during the 1948 war, during which Yerushalayim and its environs suffered extreme deprivations due to the siege laid by the Arab fighters. Conditions deteriorated to the point that there was only one available form of sustenance: grass. Specifically, there was a type of growth known by its Arab name *"khubeza,"* for which young R' Yitzchak himself would venture out to the area of Romema, where this particular grass would grow. He collected what he could, bringing the bundle home to his mother, who prepared it for consumption. Thus it was, in that period, that they ate nothing but *khubeza* grass – for breakfast, lunch, and supper.

It was not a situation, obviously, that they had sought out. But when it presented itself, they rose to the challenge, remaining steadfast in Torah and *avodah* (Divine service) throughout the protracted ordeal. Perhaps, the event may have even contributed to R' Yitzchak's own development into a most accomplished Torah figure.

לזכר ולעילוי נשמות
הירש לייב בן אברהם אהרן הלוי ע"ה
הענילא יהודית הדסה בת דוד ע"ה

NASSO

Under the Influence

THIS WEEK'S *PARSHAH* JUXTAPOSES TWO DIVERGENT sections which seem, at first glance, to have little relation to each other: Sotah and Nazir. In the first (*Bamidbar* 5:11-31), the Torah discusses the procedure of the wayward wife, whose faithfulness is suspect. She goes through a lengthy ordeal that entails the husband bringing her to the Mikdash (Sanctuary) and culminates with her drinking the "bitter waters." If she is indeed guilty, the waters inflict upon her a horrible death. In the following section (*ibid.* 6:1-21), the Torah turns its attention towards delineating the laws of the Nazir, the individual who takes a vow of abstinence from such items as grape products and haircutting.

Chazal enlighten us that there is, in fact, a common thread. This is alluded to in the Mishnah (*Sotah* 1:4), which discusses the content of the opening remarks delivered by *beis din* (the judicial court) to the suspected adulteress:

הָיוּ מַעֲלִין אוֹתָהּ לְבֵית דִּין הַגָּדוֹל שֶׁבִּירוּשָׁלַיִם, וּמְאַיְּמִין עָלֶיהָ... וְאוֹמְרִים לָהּ, בַּתִּי הַרְבֵּה יַיִן עוֹשֶׂה...

KINDLY TAKE A MOMENT TO STUDY MISHNAS CHAYIM IN THE MERIT OF
HINDA BAS HERSHEL A"H
A FELLOW JEW WHO PASSED AWAY WITH NO RELATIVES TO ARRANGE TORAH STUDY ON BEHALF OF HER *NESHAMAH*

> "They would bring her up to the Great Beis Din, which was located in Yerushalayim, and would remonstrate her... saying to her: 'My daughter, wine can result in numerous improprieties...'"

This theme is picked up by the Gemara (*Sotah* 2a), which explicitly draws the connection between these two sections: "Why is the section of the Nazir adjacent to the section of the Sotah? To tell you that whoever witnesses the Sotah in her state of degradation should abstain from wine in the manner of the Nazir." With the effects of irresponsible imbibing on full display, it would be most prudent to derive the proper lessons and restrict one's access to this pernicious agent (*cf. Rashi* to *Nazir* 2a, s.v. *"Tanna"*).

Many commentators, however, are somewhat baffled by this directive. The implication of the above teaching is that the spectacle of the Sotah's demise demands that the onlookers take precautionary measures; they must do something drastic to ensure that they don't follow her example and meet a similar fate (the paramour is also stricken through the guilty Sotah's drinking of the water [*Sotah* 27b]). But why, indeed, is this necessary? In fact, the whole notion seems somewhat counterintuitive. They have just witnessed the ordeal of the Sotah – which, put simply, was quite gruesome. She was humiliated and degraded; her ornaments were removed, and she was clothed in black; her face turned green, her eyes bulged, her veins protruded, her belly swelled and her thigh exploded (*cf. Bamidbar* 5:27; *Sotah* 7a, 20a). Who, pray tell, after seeing this, would be tempted to follow suit? "Whoever witnesses the Sotah in her state of degradation should abstain himself from wine in the manner of the Nazir"? Why bother? On the contrary, simply seeing the Sotah's demise should itself serve as the greatest deterrent for unseemly behavior. Why, then, do Chazal imply that those who observe the proceedings must take added measures (the Nazirite vow) to ensure that they don't mimic her ways?

To SHED LIGHT ON THIS ISSUE, R' YOSEF LEIB BLOCH cited the following well-known anecdote:

The Connoisseur A certain individual, a notorious alcoholic, caused his family great concern. They tried and coaxed and urged and cajoled, but to no avail.

One day it happened that a crowd gathered around an unseemly spectacle. A different man was overcome with such severe drunkenness that he lost all sense of shame. Thus he collapsed on the ground in full view, wallowing in a puddle of his own drool and vomit. The onlookers were obviously appalled by the scene, but the family of the original alcoholic saw this as a potential windfall. They ran to summon their relative, bringing him to view the abhorrent sight. They hoped that he would be so put off by the public degradation of this reprobate that it would make a forceful impression. Perhaps this would be the event to finally awaken their relative to change his ways.

But any hopes that were aroused were soon put to rest. Upon encountering the scene, their relative indeed seemed to take notice. He approached the supine drunkard, leaned over and asked him a question.

"Excuse me," he said. "I sure would like to know what did this to you. Can you tell me where I can get some?"

SUCH IS THE POTENCY OF SIN, EXPLAINED R' YOSEF Leib. Despite the horror of the consequences, the effects

Cooling Off a transgression can have on a witness can be deceptively powerful. A person may be aware of the pitfalls of sin and may even appreciate its severity. And, of course, beholding the grisly consequences can give one pause. At the same time, however, there exists another danger, one that may exert a greater influence over the beholder than the fear of punishment: that is, the mere fact that a transgression was perpetrated. The commission of a sin – and its subsequent revelation to the public – asserts an immediate effect. A person sees that the deed can be done, and so its severity, in the public's eye, is somewhat diminished.

R' Eliyahu Meir Bloch (son of R' Yosef Leib) relates the example of Amalek to illustrate this point. Chazal (*Medrash Tanchuma* §9) compare Amalek's initial attack on Yisrael to a man who jumps into a bathtub filled with scalding water. He may burn himself; but through his action, the water attains a measure of coolness. Originally, the nations were too afraid to start up with the people on whose account the Egyptians were decimated. That is, until Amalek took the initiative and fought against B'nei Yisrael. Although Amalek lost the battle, the damage was done, and the fear of Yisrael was broken. In a similar sense, when a person commits an *aveirah* (sin), he has effectively reduced the "taboo" in the eyes of the onlookers (*Peninim Mishulchan Gavohah, Bamidbar 6:2*).

The truth is, however, that the matter goes even deeper. That is, committing a sin does not carry a mere *indirect* effect, causing those with knowledge of the act to be less inhibited by the prospect of transgression. Rather – as we shall see in the coming weeks, *b'ezras Hashem* – when an *aveirah* is perpetrated, the effects on the environs are swift, direct and more powerful than we may imagine.

לזכר ולעילוי נשמת
שרה בת מנחם מנדל ע״ה

BEHA'ALOSECHA

It Can Happen to the Best of Us

PICTURE A GROUP OF WISE, ELDERLY SCHOLARS poring over their sacred tomes. These sages are the elite of their people, spending their days immersed in the ancient wisdom.

But one day, as they exit the study hall, they come across a group of children frolicking in the mud. The sages are suddenly gripped by a wild enthusiasm. Putting aside their books, they dive happily into the puddles and join the game.

After some time, the children's parents arrive; they are none too thrilled to discover their young charges covered with filth. And so they put an end to the merriment, sweeping away the mud and confiscating their digging toys. The children begin to cry. And so do the sages.

Sounds somewhat ridiculous? Possibly so. But it seems that just such a scenario takes place in this week's *parshah*. The generation that traversed the desert is known as the "*dor dei'ah*," the knowledgeable generation, distinguished for their wisdom and

---

Kindly take a moment to study Mishnas Chayim in the merit of
Tzipporah *bas* Aharon *a"h*
a fellow Jew who passed away with no relatives to arrange Torah study on behalf of her *neshamah*

elevated stature. But among them were the *eirev rav*, the mixed multitude of foreigners who would too often stir up discontent. The *passuk* relates what happened when this group lodged a complaint of alleged deprivation: "And the multitude among them asserted their desire... *and B'nei Yisrael wept as well*, crying: 'Who will provide us with meat?'" (*Bamidbar 11:4*). Rashi points out that, in truth, they had plenty of meat already, having brought numerous animals along when they left Egypt. But these people concocted an excuse to vent.

The Power of Influence

THE WHOLE EPISODE MIGHT SEEM AMAZING. HERE they were, the truly greatest generation, who witnessed Hashem's miraculous salvation; they had plenty of food, not to mention the steady supply of the wondrous *mon*, which could taste like whatever they wanted. And yet, this sagacious people were able to be persuaded by a rabble of miscreants, who spurred them to complain against Hashem for no real reason at all!

Such is the stunning power of evil influence; it can corrupt even the most elevated souls. R' Leib Chasman (*Ohr Yahel, vol. 3*) identifies the source from which is derived this fundamental notion: It is none other than the Talmudic teaching discussed last week, linking two divergent but adjoining sections in *parshas Nasso:* לָמָּה נִסְמְכָה פָּרָשַׁת נָזִיר לְפָרָשַׁת סוֹטָה? לוֹמַר לָךְ, שֶׁכָּל הָרוֹאֶה סוֹטָה בְּקִלְקוּלָהּ יַזִּיר עַצְמוֹ מִן הַיַּיִן. "Why was the section of the *Nazir* (who takes a vow to abstain from wine) placed next to the section of the *Sotah* (suspected adulteress)? To teach you that whoever witnesses the *Sotah* in her disgrace should abstain from wine" (*Sotah 2a*).

Here we are confronted with the same phenomenon, as implied by Chazal's precise wording. They did not state simply הָרוֹאֶה סוֹטָה בְּקִלְקוּלָהּ – "**One** who sees a *Sotah* in her disgrace," but rather כָּל הָרוֹאֶה סוֹטָה בְּקִלְקוּלָהּ – "**All** who see a *Sotah* in her disgrace." The emphasis on "*kol*," explains R' Leib, is intended to include even those individuals of extraordinary spiritual stature. A person could have thought that he would be effectively immune from negative influence, given his heightened spiritual fortitude. This is especially so in light of the fact that he was witness to the debasement and demise of the *Sotah* – a gruesome sight for anyone to behold. Nevertheless, even such a person is enjoined to take precautionary measures for the future, having been exposed, however minimally, to the incidence of sin. In the end, no one is entirely inured from evil influence; the Mishnah (*Avos* 2:4) warns that no one, ever, may rest on his laurels:

אַל תַּאֲמֵן בְּעַצְמְךָ עַד יוֹם מוֹתָךְ.

"Do not be assured of your spiritual status – until the day of your passing."

Cold Turkey

R' YA'AKOV NEIMAN (*DARCHEI MUSSAR, PARSHAS Ki Seitzei*) relates a real-life example of the above. A great man underwent a spiritual downfall, and another sage, upon learning about his fate, decided to put Chazal's exhortation into practice.

It began with a commotion in the street; a gaggle of gawking children were gathered in a circle. As children are wont to do, they were engaged in raucous behavior, hurling stones at something in the middle of the circle. The object of the children's scorn was a man, stone-drunk, lolling around on the floor and murmuring incessantly. What was most surprising (or disconcerting) about this scene was that the statements issuing forth from his mouth were neither imprecations against his attackers or even regular drunken driver. Rather, he was mumbling *divrei Torah*, sacred and scholarly thoughts and statements.

Word of this incident reached the ears of R' Simchah Zissel Ziv, the great *mussar* figure known as the Alter from Kelm. Upon looking into the matter, he learned, to his chagrin, that the man was indeed a formidable *talmid chacham* (Torah scholar) who of late had fallen into some extremely bad habits.

R' Simchah Zissel was shocked and appalled by this first-hand demonstration of the power of (being under the) influence. Here was a man, a great Torah scholar, whose stature and life were destroyed through an addiction to alcohol.

On the spot, he took Chazal's teaching to heart – "*yazir atzmo min hayayin*" – he should abstain from drinking wine. Referring to the offending alcoholic beverage, R' Simchah Zissel pronounced: "It will never again appear on my table" (*Peninim Mishulchan Gavohah, Parshas Nasso*).

The above reveals to us the immense danger inherent in sin, how its very existence can draw in even the most elevated people. And this can occur even when the disastrous consequences of transgression are on full display. What yet remains to explore, however, are the precise mechanics. What, indeed, is the source of this power? How does it exert such a forceful pull, even in the midst of such adverse circumstances? This issue, *b'ezras Hashem*, will be addressed more fully next week.

לזכר ולעילוי נשמות
משה דוד בן יחזקאל ע"ה
צירל בת שמעון ע"ה

SHELACH

Warning: Flammable!

THE ESTEEM IN WHICH MOSHE RABBEINU HELD Yehoshua, his prime disciple, is evident from the opening statement of Pirkei Avos (*1:1*):

מֹשֶׁה קִבֵּל תּוֹרָה מִסִּינַי, וּמְסָרָהּ לִיהוֹשֻׁעַ.

"Moshe received the Torah from Sinai and transmitted it to Yehoshua."

From all the members of that exalted generation, it was Yehoshua who was entrusted with the pre-eminent task of safeguarding the very Torah given at Har Sinai, and to pass it down, unaltered, to future generations. His selection is a testament to his stature, erudition and trustworthiness.

IT WOULD APPEAR SOMEWHAT STRANGE, THEN, THAT Moshe had to offer the specific prayer that he did in this week's

Model of Consistency parshah. The *passuk* makes mention of the name-change Moshe accorded to his disciple: וַיִּקְרָא מֹשֶׁה לְהוֹשֵׁעַ בִּן־נוּן יְהוֹשֻׁעַ - "And Moshe called Hoshei'a bin Nun (by the name of) 'Yehoshua'" (*Bamidbar*

Kindly take a moment to study Mishnas Chayim in the merit of
Soroh Leah bas Moshe Yosef HaLevi a"h
A fellow Jew who passed away with no relatives to arrange Torah study on behalf of her *Neshamah*

13:16). Rashi explains the significance of this adjustment: It reflects Moshe's prayer on Yehoshua's behalf. The first two letters of this name signify a Name of Hashem, while the remainder is from the root-word for salvation (*yeshu'ah*). Thus Moshe solicited Hashem's deliverance, saying: קָהּ יוֹשִׁיעֲךָ מֵעֲצַת מְרַגְּלִים – "May Hashem save you from the design of the spies."

What was it, exactly, that Moshe was worried about? Did he fear that his eminent disciple, reliable enough to be entrusted with the transmission of the entire Torah, would fall into collaboration with the spies (who later turned the people against Hashem)? R' Simchah Zissel Ziv, the Alter of Kelm, points to this as yet another example of the far and pernicious reach of the power of evil. As was discussed last week, no matter how great is one's stature, no one is immune from the allure of its influence. Chazal had warned that "***Kol haro'eh***," "**all** who see" the disgrace of a *Sotah* (suspected adulteress), must distance themselves from drinking wine; these protective measures apply to **anyone**, even the most elevated souls. And so even someone on the level of Yehoshua was at risk of falling under the spell of evil influence (*Yalkut Lekach Tov*).

(Interestingly enough, this is the same R' Simchah Zissel who was featured last week in the incident of the scholarly drunkard. Upon learning that a certain Torah scholar had descended into alcoholism, R' Simchah Zissel, then and there, unequivocally proscribed the drinking of wine, stating that it would never again grace his table.)

QUITE A REMARKABLE PICTURE EMERGES FROM OUR study of the *parshiyos* over the last few weeks.

Igniting Evil
We have seen, for instance, the concern Chazal had for the witnesses to the *Sotah's* ordeal. The *Sotah* had to undergo humiliation and disgrace, and the consequences of her impropriety were a horrible and public death. And yet there was still a fear that the onlookers could be tempted to follow her example, to the point that it was necessary for them to forswear drinking wine! This was a concern not only

for common folk; even someone of impeccable righteousness was considered at risk. Apparently, the exposure to the mere fact that someone had perpetrated a sin was enough to create a danger that others would replicate the deed. How, indeed, are we to understand this phenomenon?

One proffered explanation attributed the concern to a matter of "desensitization." Following the model of Amalek, once one nation attacked Yisrael, others would be emboldened to follow suit. So it is with sin – the perpetrator has demonstrated, in some sense, that sin is an "option," which somewhat diminishes the inhibitions of the onlookers.

According to R' Reuvein Grozovsky, however, the matter goes much deeper. Imbued with an evil inclination, man possesses an inherent *netiyah* (propensity) toward vice. He illustrates this idea with a comparison to fire. For most objects to catch fire, actual contact is necessary. Even a twig, for example, needs to be placed firmly within a fire; it may even be held there for a few moments before the flame actually catches. But then there are items that are highly flammable. For example, a match contains, within its head, a certain chemical combination that makes it highly susceptible to ignition. As such, it is not necessary to even place the match within the actual fire; when it simply draws near to the heat, the head bursts into flame. And so it is with the evil inclination. It is primed for sin; when it simply draws near transgression, it is ready to ignite. The slightest exposure will set it off (*Peninim Mishulchan Gavohah, Parshas Nasso*).

R' Leib Chasman – whose initial comments on this issue were cited last week – draws a parallel to our own lives. A wizened old sage, pristine and elevated, beholds a *Sotah* one time in the throes of her disgraceful ordeal. Nevertheless, he is in spiritual danger and must take unequivocal measures to avoid future pitfalls. How much more so, then, must we be vigilant, for we witness myriad transgressors and free-thinkers on a daily basis – people who condone and perpetrate all manner of deeds that run contrary to Torah values. And unlike the *Sotah*, who suffers humiliation and is held in universal contempt, these individuals dress up their deeds and ideas in all sorts of "sophisticated" terminology, such as "progressivism" and the like. Surely, then, we must apply safeguards upon being subjected to exposure of such outlandish behavior and attitudes.

What is supremely chilling about R' Leib's remarks is that they were made roughly one hundred years ago, and he was referring to his environs, the backwoods of Lithuanian *shtetls*! Continuing with his train of thought, then, we must extend his *kal vachomer* to our times: If such can be said about the Lithuanian streets of 100 years ago, how much more so must we, in the twenty-first century, surrounded by the cesspools of secularism and liberal hedonism, be attuned to the ever-present spiritual dangers. Certainly, it behooves us, as much as possible, to refrain from even approaching the fire.

לזכר ולעילוי נשמת
אברהם בן עזרא ע"ה

KORACH

Where in the World...?

THE RAMBAN IN HIS ESSAY *SHA'AR HAGEMUL* WRITES the following: "Being that it is explicit from the teachings of our Sages that final retribution is meted out in Gehinnom... it behooves us to clarify, based on their words, what the nature of this punishment called 'Gehinnom' is..." In his work, the Ramban proceeds to elaborate with some detail on the nature of both Gehinnom and Gan Eden and the gamut of the concept of Divine reward and punishment. An incident related to this week's *parshah* affords us the opportunity, however minimally, to fulfill the Ramban's aforementioned dictum, which we will seek to do largely by drawing from his very words.

THE INCIDENT REFERRED TO INVOLVES THE DESCENT to the depths of the participants in Korach's rebellion, concerning whom it states (*Bamidbar 16:33*): וַיֵּרְדוּ הֵם וְכָל־אֲשֶׁר לָהֶם חַיִּים שְׁאֹלָה – "And they, and all that was to them, descended, while living, to the netherworld." R' Eliyahu Dushnitzer remarked on the extent of this precipitous plunge. The Yerushalmi relates (*Sanhedrin 10:4*)

How Low Can One Go?

KINDLY TAKE A MOMENT TO STUDY MISHNAS CHAYIM IN THE MERIT OF
ROCHEL *BAS* **NOSSON** *A"H*
A FELLOW JEW WHO PASSED AWAY WITH NO RELATIVES TO ARRANGE TORAH STUDY ON BEHALF OF HER *NESHAMAH*

that the transgressors continued to fall farther and farther until the righteous Chanah offered prayers on their behalf. What is most remarkable about this is the sheer amount of time that elapsed. Korach's followers were sucked into the earth circa (the Jewish year) 2450; Chanah offered her prayer circa 2830. This means that the rebels were falling steadily downward for almost 400 years – and would have gone even further, if not for Chanah's merciful intercession (*cf. Derech Sichah* [*R' Chaim Kanievsky*]).

What is especially chilling from this account is the revelation of Gehinnom's mammoth dimensions. Gehinnom is comprised of seven levels, one below the next. According to the Tannaic work "*Orko Shel Olam*" (cited by the Ramban), the span of each level is quite large: it would take 300 years to traverse any one of them. This means, then, that Korach's swallowed multitude had barely cleared the first level by the time of Chanah's prayer, and without it would have continued falling for another 1,700 years. This means they would have hit rock-bottom roughly around the time of the reign of Charlemagne.

While the fact that Gehinnom is accorded specific dimensions may come as a surprise to many, the Ramban is fairly unequivocal on this point. While asserting that there should be no real need to bring extensive supporting evidence – as the matter is already quite explicit in the Gemara and *medrashim* – the Ramban, in fact, does proceed to cite various sources at some length (apparently to starkly negate the cynics and apostates). Thus he quotes the Talmudic teaching (*Eruvin 19a*) that identifies three points on earth that contain an entranceway to Gehinnom: Yerushalayim, (somewhere) in the sea, and in the desert (the latter being derived from the earlier-cited *passuk* from this week's *parshah*: וַיֵּרְדוּ הֵם וְכָל־אֲשֶׁר לָהֶם חַיִּים שְׁאֹלָה). Another example is a passage from the *Medrash Iggeres* (*Epistle of*) *R' Yehoshua ben Levi*, which contains a vivid portrayal of the sage R' Yehoshua ben Levi's observations upon his visit to Gehinnom, in which he took some actual measurements: "When I measured the first house in (one of the) levels, I found it to be 100 *mil* in length and 50 *mil* in width (approx.

70 miles x 35 miles)." After various such citations, the Ramban concludes: "These and similar matters should not be relegated to mere allegory, for (Chazal) have detailed the location... and have even derived *halachic* ramifications (from some of the delineated details)..."

Perfect Fit

ONE ISSUE THAT ARISES, HOWEVER, RELATES TO ONE of the citations the Ramban himself brings. Regarding the measurement of these areas, the Gemara (*Ta'anis 10a*) engages in some comparisons: "The world is 1/60th the size of Gan Eden; Gan Eden is 1/60th the size of Eden itself; and Eden is 1/60th the size of Gehinnom. Thus, the entire world, in comparison to Gehinnom, resembles a lid covering a cauldron." The obvious question is a practical one: Gehinnom, the Ramban explained, is an actual location contained on this earth, as is Gan Eden (the Ramban cites an opinion [that of the Ibn Ezra] that it is located "under the equator"). But how is this possible? If Gan Eden is sixty times greater than the earth's area, and Gehinnom is even larger than that – how could the world possibly contain these entities?

The *Chazon Yo'el* (commentary to the *Sha'ar Hagemul*; §376) posits that the issue is comparable to a phenomenon found in the Beis Hamikdash. Commenting on the remarkable spiritual qualities of the *Aron Hakodesh* (Holy Ark), the Gemara (*Bava Basra 99a*) tells us that, while placed squarely within the *Kodesh Hakadashim* (Holy of Holies), the *Aron* itself took up no physical space. That is, the Torah delineates the dimensions of the *Aron* as being 2½ cubits long. It was placed within a chamber that itself was 20 cubits wide. What would happen if one were to measure from each side of the *Aron* to its adjacent wall? Mathematical law would render that the measurer should discover a span of 8.75 cubits on either side (8.75 x 2 + 2.5 = 20). But what actually happened is that one would measure a span of 10 cubits on either side! Apparently, being an inherently spiritual object, it did not register as taking up space in the physical realm. These could also be the attributes of Gehinnom and Gan Eden; only one (such as R' Yehoshua ben

Levi) who could gain access to them would be able to observe their measurements; but on this physical world, they do not take up actual space.

One point the Ramban adds is that while the matters and details he discusses (regarding Gehinnom and Gan Eden) are to be taken quite literally, they do serve a dual purpose. "All of these matters," he writes, "Gan Eden, its four rivers, the Tree of Life, the Tree of Knowledge, etc., exist exactly as stated... but they also help to illustrate another deeper, more esoteric matter." The Ramban compares the situation to an aspect of the examination of the witnesses for the new moon, as stated in the Mishnah (*Rosh Hashanah 2:8*):

> דְּמוּת צוּרוֹת לְבָנוֹת הָיוּ לוֹ לְרַבָּן גַּמְלִיאֵל בַּטַּבְלָא וּבַכֹּתֶל בַּעֲלִיָּתוֹ, שֶׁבָּהֶן מַרְאֶה אֶת הַהֶדְיוֹטוֹת וְאוֹמֵר, הֲכָזֶה רָאִיתָ אוֹ כָזֶה?

> *"Rabban Gamliel had images of moon shapes on a tablet on the wall of his attic, which he used to display to the simple folk (who arrived bearing testimony that they had witnessed the new moon). (To verify their claim) he would say to them: 'Did it appear like this or like that?'"*

These visual aids of Rabban Gamliel were real, of course, but they served a purpose of illustrating the more vast entity that was the heavenly bodies. In a similar sense, the Torah and Chazal have revealed to us certain aspects of the Next World, which exist in their literal form. At the same time, they reflect much deeper entities, matters that cannot be fully grasped by mortal comprehension and whose true nature is more spectacular than our wildest dreams.

לזכר ולעילוי נשמת

יהודה לייב ע״ה בן מאיר ואסתר נ״י

CHUKAS

The Complete Cow

ONE OF THE DEVICES EMPLOYED TO MAKE *halachic* determinations is the notion of "*rov* (majority)," whereby a matter of doubt can be resolved by considering and drawing from the majority of relevant cases. This idea can be illustrated by the classic Talmudic discussion (*Chullin 11a*), which seeks the source for this rule. It finds it from none other than the section of the *parah adumah* (red cow), featured in the beginning of this week's *parshah*.

THE DISCUSSION BEGINS BY CITING THE VERSES THAT highlight some key steps in the process of preparing the *parah adumah* for ritual use: וּנְתַתֶּם אֹתָהּ אֶל־אֶלְעָזָר הַכֹּהֵן וְהוֹצִיא אֹתָהּ אֶל־מִחוּץ לַמַּחֲנֶה **וְשָׁחַט** אֹתָהּ לְפָנָיו... **וְשָׂרַף** אֶת־הַפָּרָה לְעֵינָיו. "And you shall

Fragile – Don't Dissect

give (the cow) to Elazar the Kohein, and he shall remove it to outside the camp, and it shall be **slaughtered** before him... And it shall be burned before his eyes" (*Bamidbar 19:3-5*). The Gemara makes a derivation from the juxtaposition of these highlighted

---

KINDLY TAKE A MOMENT TO STUDY MISHNAS CHAYIM IN THE MERIT OF
CHAYAH BAS YEHUDAH A"H
A FELLOW JEW WHO PASSED AWAY WITH NO RELATIVES TO ARRANGE TORAH STUDY ON BEHALF OF HER *NESHAMAH*

actions, which intimates that they must share a common quality. Thus it learns that just as the animal is whole when it is brought to slaughter, so must the burning process be initiated on a complete animal. That is, one may not, for example, alter the body of the cow prior to burning.

This leads to a certain difficulty. By viewing the cow prior to its burning, one can determine with relative ease that its body is complete. But what about the *internals*? There are numerous contingencies of internal blemish that could render the animal "incomplete" and thus disqualified. These are known as *"tereifos"* and are listed (in the context of the laws of *kashrus*) in the Mishnah in Chullin (*3:1*), which states:

אֵלּוּ טְרֵפוֹת בַּבְּהֵמָה, נְקוּבַת הַוֵּשֶׁט, וּפְסוּקַת הַגַּרְגֶּרֶת, נִקַּב קְרוּם שֶׁל מֹחַ...

"The following are the disqualifying blemishes of an animal (rendering it unfit for consumption): A puncture of the esophagus, a slit in the windpipe, a hole in the brain membrane..."

The Mishnah proceeds to list a total of eighteen *tereifos*. This would seem to present a problem with regard to the burning of the *parah adumah*; how do we know that it doesn't contain, for example, a punctured esophagus or brain membrane? Dissecting the animal and conducting an "internal investigation" (as is done in processing meat for consumption) is out of the question here, for as stated, the burning must be conducted on a complete animal; the dissection itself would cause its disqualification.

And so, the Gemara concludes, it must be that we rely on the *rov* (that's "majority," not "rabbi." We rely on him, too, but that's more conventionally transliterated as *"rav." "Rov"* rhymes with "drove." In any event...). That is, the majority of cows in the world are free from these internal *tereifos*; seeing as in the case of *parah adumah* we can't examine its innards, we may assume that this particular specimen shares the same constitution as the majority of its bovine colleagues.

A brief synopsis of this fairly involved Talmudic analysis could be stated as follows: We learn that the *parah adumah* must remain whole up to the point of its burning; we question how we can be sure it is in fact "complete," given the possibility of internal *tereifos*; opening up the animal for examination is not an option as this itself renders the animal incomplete; we answer that it must be that we are sanctioned to assume, in accordance with the majority of cases, that the animal's internals are unblemished. Hence, *parah adumah* is a source for the rule of "*rov*," ruling by the majority.

The Era of Transparency

AN ISSUE ARISES, HOWEVER, WHEN WE REVIEW THE comments of the Targum Yonasan ben Uziel to the abovementioned passage. On the *passuk* that states that the cow was given over to the jurisdiction of Elazar Hakohein (*Bamidbar* 19:3), the Targum Yonasan states explicitly: וְיִבְדְקִינֵיהּ בְּתַמְנֵי סְרֵי טְרֵיפָן – "And he shall examine it for the eighteen (forms of) *tereifus*"! This seems to run completely counter to the Gemara's entire discussion, which starkly ruled out such examination on the grounds that it would detract from the "wholeness" of the *parah*!

Drawing on some fascinating background information, the *Sheilos U'teshuvos Beis Yitzchak* (*Yoreh Dei'ah* §39) offers a brilliant resolution. Tosafos in Shabbos (*22b*), citing the Beraisa D'meleches Hamishkan, supplies some insight on the situation of B'nei Yisrael in the desert. As is known, they were accompanied by the *Amud He'anan* (Pillar of Cloud) throughout their travels. Apparently, this cloud, aside from offering protection, also provided them with light – a light so bright that they were literally able to see through walls. Thus, they could peer, for example, at a sealed barrel, and be able to view its internal contents.

Armed with this information, the *Beis Yitzchak* resolves the apparent contradiction between the Gemara in Chullin and the comments of the Targum Yonasan. Thanks to the "transparent view" provided by the *Amud He'anan*, Elazar Hakohein had the wherewithal to examine the *parah adumah* for *tereifos* without having to make a single incision. By its light, he simply looked at the complete cow and viewed its internal organs. The Gemara that ruled out checking for *tereifos* – necessitating, instead, to rely on the rule of *rov* – was referring to *parah adumahs* of successive generations, which did not have the benefit of utilizing the *Anan's* light. The Targum Yonasan, however, was commenting directly on the verse that mentions Elazar Hakohein. As he officiated during the Jews' sojourn in the desert, the offices of the *Amud He'anan* were readily at his disposal.

לזכר ולעילוי נשמת
הרה"ח ר' מאיר בן ר' ישראל זצ"ל

BALAK

Bilam and
(L'havdil Elef v'alfei Havdalos)
R' Yose ben Kisma

ONE OF THE AREAS WHEREBY CHAZAL EMPHASIZE Bilam's low character and nefarious motives takes place near the beginning of this week's *parshah*. Balak King of Moav, intent on solving his "Jewish Problem", reaches out to Bilam the prophet/sorceror/imprecation expext to place a curse on B'nei Yisrael. Bilam confers with the Almighty, Who (initially) informs him to refuse the request. Balak persists in his request, to which Bilam responds (*Bamidbar* 22:18): אִם־יִתֶּן־לִי בָלָק מְלֹא בֵיתוֹ כֶּסֶף וְזָהָב לֹא אוּכַל לַעֲבֹר אֶת־פִּי ד' – "(Even) if Balak were to give me his entire house filled with silver and gold, I would not be able to transgress the command of Hashem." While on the surface everything may seem kosher, in fact, the inference indicates the opposite. As Rashi states (*ibid.*): "From here we see that he possessed an avaricious nature, craving the wealth of others." In referring to this "house filled with silver and gold", Bilam revealed where his eyes and heart really lay.

KINDLY TAKE A MOMENT TO STUDY MISHNAS CHAYIM IN THE MERIT OF
LEIB BEN DOVID A"H
A FELLOW JEW WHO PASSED AWAY WITH NO RELATIVES TO ARRANGE TORAH STUDY ON BEHALF OF HIS *NESHAMAH*

THE ISSUE THE COMMENTATORS POINT TO IS THAT there appears to be a similar incident, recorded in Pirkei Avos.

Same Answer, Different Meanings

Only here, the protagonist, R' Yose ben Kisma, is heralded as a selfless *tzaddik* (righteous individual) willing to sacrifice everything for what's right. In the Mishnah (6:9), R' Yose relates his encounter:

> פַּעַם אַחַת הָיִיתִי מְהַלֵּךְ בַּדֶּרֶךְ וּפָגַע בִּי אָדָם אֶחָד, וְנָתַן לִי שָׁלוֹם, וְהֶחֱזַרְתִּי לוֹ שָׁלוֹם, אָמַר לִי, רַבִּי, מֵאֵיזֶה מָקוֹם אַתָּה, אָמַרְתִּי לוֹ, מֵעִיר גְּדוֹלָה שֶׁל חֲכָמִים וְשֶׁל סוֹפְרִים אָנִי, אָמַר לִי, רַבִּי רְצוֹנְךָ שֶׁתָּדוּר עִמָּנוּ בִּמְקוֹמֵנוּ וַאֲנִי אֶתֵּן לְךָ אֶלֶף אֲלָפִים דִּינְרֵי זָהָב וַאֲבָנִים טוֹבוֹת וּמַרְגָּלִיּוֹת, אָמַרְתִּי לוֹ אִם אַתָּה נוֹתֵן לִי כָּל כֶּסֶף וְזָהָב וַאֲבָנִים טוֹבוֹת וּמַרְגָּלִיּוֹת שֶׁבָּעוֹלָם, אֵינִי דָר אֶלָּא בִּמְקוֹם תּוֹרָה.

"One time, I was going along the way when I met up with a certain man. He greeted me with 'Shalom', and I returned the greeting. He said to me: 'Rebbi, from what place do you hail?' I said to him: 'I am from a great city of wise men and scholars.' He said to me: 'Rebbi, would you like to dwell with us in our location? If so, I will give you millions of gold coins, precious stones, and pearls.' I said to him: 'If you were to give me all of the silver, gold, precious stones, and pearls that exist in the world, I still would choose to live only in a place of Torah!'"

At first glance, R' Yose's reply to his supplicant is reminiscent of Bilam's response to Balak. Like the gentile prophet, R' Yose also states that he can't betray his principles – "not for all the money in the world." Yet, no one accuses R' Yose of trying to pass on any hints. What, indeed, is the difference? They seemed to have expressed the same sentiment; yet in one case, Chazal detect an undercurrent of greed, while in the other, they have nothing but high praise!

One could have suggested (as some do; *cf. Emes L'Ya'akov* to Avos 6:9, footnote 176) that there is not necessarily any significant difference in the formulation of their answers; rather, Chazal accurately interpreted their respective intentions based on their inherent nature. The Mishnah elsewhere in Avos (*5:19*) states that Bilam possessed a "*nefesh rechavah*" (craving soul); based on this knowledge, it stands to reason that his answer was dictated by his greed. R' Yose ben Kisma, who is known for his piety, surely did not harbor such coarse intentions.

However, as stated, Rashi intimates that the order was reversed; that is, it was from Bilam's response that Chazal inferred that he was a covetous individual. Apparently, Rashi detected some distinction in the actual wording of their answer which accounted for the opposing assessments. The question remains, then: what was the difference?

Know Your Man

R' YA'AKOV KAMENETSKY (*EMES L'YA'AKOV, IBID.*) points out a concrete distinction. True, in both refusals, both stated that even a large sum of money wouldn't make them change their minds. The difference lay in the feasibility of their "non-offer". Notice Bilam's careful wording, in which he utilized defined and limited terminology: "(Even) if Balak were to give me *his entire house* filled with silver and gold, I would not be able to transgress the command of Hashem." That's only one house of which Bilam was speaking. But he left room for a counter-offer. "Okay, you won't do it for one gold-filled house. But maybe if we threw in a second or third treasure-filled structure..." That's where Bilam was hoping the conversation would turn. But R' Yose ben Kisma was unequivocal: "Even if you were to give me all of the silver, gold, precious stones, and pearls that exist in the world, I still would choose to live only in a place of Torah!" That basically covers it all. R' Yose obviously would brook no compromise.

Perhaps we may suggest another approach, based on an observation of the Maharal (*Derech Hachaim*). Where did Chazal perceive the difference? Perhaps their assessment came not so much from a distinction in the formulation of their response, but rather from the nature of *the individuals who were making the offering*. In Bilam's case, he was dealing with Balak, a would-be employer of flesh-and-blood. Bilam had no reason to expect that Balak was making anything other than a serious offer. And so Bilam knew he had someone with whom to negotiate. As such, he tried to drive a hard bargain.

But the encounter of R' Yose ben Kisma was a different matter. "One time, I was going along the way when I met up with a certain man." Who was this mysterious figure? According to the Maharal, it was none other than the *yetzer hara*, come to try and tempt R' Yose away from the proper path.

This is where Chazal saw to draw a distinction. It became apparent that R' Yose was on to the stranger's identity and plan. He realized he wasn't dealing with a regular "negotiating partner" looking to close a deal. As opposed to Bilam, then, when he insisted he would not betray his ideals for the promise of wealth – he really meant it.

לזכר ולעילוי נשמות
אפרים בן משה הכהן ע"ה
מלכה בת הערשל ע"ה

PINCHAS

Pinchas and Zimri: The Ironic Climax

THIS WEEK'S *PARSHAH* RELATES HOW THE TRIBAL leader Zimri, acting in a renegade and defiant fashion, was killed by Pinchas. The contrast is stark, as Zimri is deplored for the indiscretion for which he was condemned to die, while the Torah lauds Pinchas, on whom was bestowed eternal priesthood in recognition of his deed. The duration of this dramatic encounter, it would seem, was quite short, a matter of a few eventful moments. In truth, though, it was the culmination of a long and ironic story which, as we shall see, was actually hundreds of years in the making.

PERHAPS MORE THAN ANY OF THE OTHER *SHEVATIM* (tribes), Shimon and Levi were a real pair. This is evident from the **Together from the Start** Torah's description of an occurrence on the brothers' return journey from Mitzrayim (Egypt) to their father's house. Having just purchased grain in Mitzrayim (where Shimon was incarcerated),

---

Kindly take a moment to study Mishnas Chayim in the merit of
Yehudah *ben* Ephraim HaLevi *a"h*
a fellow Jew who passed away with no relatives to arrange Torah study on behalf of his *neshamah*

one of them made a frightening discovery: the purchasing money had been returned to his sack. As the *passuk* states (*Bereishis 42:27*): וַיִּפְתַּח הָאֶחָד אֶת־שַׂקּוֹ... וַיַּרְא אֶת־כַּסְפּוֹ וְהִנֵּה־הוּא בְּפִי אַמְתַּחְתּוֹ – "And **the one** opened his sack... and saw his money, for behold! It was in the mouth of his sack." Rashi identifies "the one" as Levi, explaining that he was referred to by this appellation "for he remained alone (as one) from Shimon, his natural partner."

Apparently, the two were inseparable – for better or otherwise. This point was made by their father, Ya'akov; when granting his final blessing to his sons, he actually delivered an admonition to this pair, stating at the outset: "*Shimon v'Levi achim* – Shimon and Levi are brothers" (*ibid. 49:5*). This might seem like an unusual statement; isn't it obvious that they were brothers? Rashi explains that their father was emphasizing their quality of plotting together, such as in the attempt to rid themselves of Yosef and in planning the attack on the city of Shechem.

Thus, their paths began with a special closeness. Even in later years, we find that the tribes that descended from them were alike in a number of ways. They both had smaller populations in comparison to the other *shevatim*. And they both essentially lacked a distinct portion in Eretz Yisrael that they could call their own. Concerning the tribe of Shimon, the *passuk* says (*Yehoshua 19:1*): "And their portion was in the midst of the portion of Yehudah." Levi was also only granted sporadic cities spread throughout the portions of the other tribes. All of this was in fulfillment of Ya'akov's charge: "I will divide them among (the Land of) Ya'akov and scatter them in Yisrael" (*Bereishis 49:7*).

But even within these similarities, we begin to notice some distinctions. Both of them lacked established portions in Eretz Yisrael – but for different reasons. For Shimon, the cause seems to have been simply a result of Ya'akov's decree. Regarding Levi, however, we find an additional, more elevated calculation; as the *passuk* states (*Bamidbar 18:20*): "**Hashem** is their portion."

Their comparatively small population also resulted from different causes. In the case of Levi, it seems to have been a technical factor.

Most of the nation proliferated exponentially in Mitzrayim. But there was a prerequisite for such accelerated propagation: the oppressive bondage. As the *passuk* states (*Shemos 1:12*): "And as much as (the Egyptians) would afflict them, so would (the Jewish nation) increase and multiply." The tribe of Levi was exempt from the enslavement and so were not included in the population explosion. The tribe of Shimon, who were enslaved, did initially attain a large population. But this was later diminished due to the unfortunate events connected to the act of Zimri (tribal leader of *shevet* Shimon) mentioned in this week's *parshah*. In addition to Zimri's demise, thousands of his fellow tribesmen were decimated by the plague Hashem inflicted on those who were similarly led astray.

Are You Paying Attention?

THUS WE HAVE A SOMEWHAT TRAGIC STORY THAT developed over time. Two brothers from the most elevated Jewish household – themselves of exalted spiritual status – began as a steadfast pair. But over the years, as evidenced by the actions and situations of their progeny, their paths clearly diverged in separate directions. All of this culminates in this week's *parshah*, as the righteous scion of Levi, Pinchas, killed the rebellious scion of the house of Shimon. What happened? Perhaps we can gain some insight from the following anecdote:

The story is told of two *chavrusas* (study partners) who had been studying a *masechta* (tractate) together for some time. One of them arrived one day at the daily session and began placing food items on the table. His partner saw that a platter of cake and *shnapps* had materialized next to their *Gemaras*. His face took on a quizzical look, leading to the following exchange:

CHAVRUSA # 1: "What's all this for?"

CHAVRUSA # 2: "Oh, a *siyum* (celebration upon completing a volume)."

1: "A *siyum*? Who's making a *siyum*?"

2: "What do you mean, 'Who's making a *siyum*?' We are!"

1: "A *siyum*? But we're only up to *daf lamed daled* (page 34)!"

2: "I know! That's why we're making a *siyum* – it's the last page!"

1: "The last page? No it's not! *Daf kuf hei* (page 105) is!"

2: "What are you talking about? *Maseches Erchin* only goes up to *daf lamed daled*!"

1: "*Erchin*? We're learning *Eruvin*!"

Two people (allegedly) studying together; but paying attention really makes a difference!

R' Shimon Schwab (*Mayan Beis Hasho'eivah, Parshas Vayechi*) explains the divergent life-courses of Shimon and Levi in a similar fashion. As mentioned, their father delivered an admonished the both of them, simultaneously. It seems, however, that – judging on a standard corresponding to their elevated spiritual status – Levi took the matter more to heart.

While we might not always appreciate constructive criticism or a "*mussar-schmooze*," Chazal encourage us to accept – and even desire – such exhortations to improvement. This quality is listed in the Mishnah in Avos (6:6) as one of the preconditions for acquiring Torah:

הַתּוֹרָה נִקְנֵית בְּאַרְבָּעִים וּשְׁמוֹנָה דְבָרִים. וְאֵלוּ הֵן... אוֹהֵב אֶת הַתּוֹכָחוֹת.

"*Torah is acquired through forty-eight items, including... loving (to receive) reproof.*"

It can be challenging to be receptive to rebuke. But from the above, we see the vast difference that exists between one who takes the matter to heart... and one who does not.

לזכר ולעילוי נשמת
שלמה שלום בן יעקב מרדכי ע"ה

MATOS-MASEI

Secrets of Masei

IF YOU'VE EVER LOOKED AT A MAP OF A COUNTRY like Egypt or Saudi Arabia (if you haven't, you're not missing much), you might notice something curious: Although the landmass is quite large, most of the cities are clustered around a relative tiny portion of the country (the Nile River, in Egypt's case). There is a good reason for this: the huge uninhabited portion is by and large just barren desert.

THIS IS ONE OF THE INTRIGUING FACTORS OF THIS week's *parshah*. The beginning section of *parshas* Masei is comprised, for the most part, of names: a lengthy list of all the places to which B'nei Yisrael traveled while sojourning in the desert – which gives rise to a few obvious questions: Why would such a seemingly insignificant swath of land be replete with so many named locations? And why would the Torah, known for its extremely conservative word usage, expend so much space just listing place after place through which the people passed in their travels?

The Itinerary

KINDLY TAKE A MOMENT TO STUDY MISHNAS CHAYIM IN THE MERIT OF
LEIB BEN ELIYOHU A"H
A FELLOW JEW WHO PASSED AWAY WITH NO RELATIVES TO ARRANGE TORAH STUDY ON BEHALF OF HIS *NESHAMAH*

The issue is somewhat compounded further by the practice in many congregations, when reading this section from the Torah, to adopt the joyous reading-tune employed for certain key passages such as *Az Yashir*. Publicly reading the hymn of praise offered by Yisrael after their deliverance from Mitzrayim (Egypt) would appropriately occasion the use of such a triumphant tune. But why, exactly, is the listing of various, seemingly insignificant travel-stops the cause for glorious celebration?

To gain insight into this issue, R' Moshe Shternbuch (*Ta'am V'da'as*) draws our attention to a somewhat mysterious passage from the Mishnah. (Prior to its elucidation, we will first cite the passage and provide a more straightforward translation.) The Mishnah states (*Eduyos 2:9*):

> וּבְמִסְפַּר הַדּוֹרוֹת... וְהוּא הַקֵּץ, שֶׁנֶּאֱמַר קֹרֵא הַדֹּרוֹת מֵרֹאשׁ, אַף עַל פִּי שֶׁנֶּאֱמַר וַעֲבָדוּם וְעִנּוּ אֹתָם אַרְבַּע מֵאוֹת שָׁנָה, וְנֶאֱמַר וְדוֹר רְבִיעִי יָשׁוּבוּ הֵנָּה.

> *"And in the number of generations... and the ending date. As it states (Yeshayah 41:4), 'He summons the generations from the beginning.' Even though it states (Bereishis 15:13), 'And they will enslave and oppress them for 400 years,' it also states (ibid. v. 16), 'and the fourth generation will return here.'"*

Double Deadlines

THE COMMENTATORS GO TO GREAT LENGTHS TO clarify these enigmatic words. The Ra'avad explains this passage in a most interesting way, seeing the Mishnah as setting forth a foundational principle in the workings of *galus v'ge'ulah* (exile and redemption). When a Heavenly decree is promulgated regarding a given exile, two separate dates will be advanced to signify the time-duration; one will be expressed in numbers of years, the other through generations. The Mishnah provides the example of the Egyptian exile. The Torah states that the bondage will last for *400 years*, but it also mentions that the exiles will return after *four generations*.

How could there be two deadlines? The Ra'avad explains that even when the exile itself and its associated persecution has elapsed, this does not automatically translate into redemption. The actual deliverance arrives at a later date. As such, the bondage in Mitzrayim ended at the end of the 400-year period. But the full redemption did not take place until forty years later, when the fourth generation returned to the Land.

A similar phenomenon, the Ra'avad continues, was manifest in the Babylonian exile. The exile itself lasted for seventy years; but even as the exiles came back, the redemption was not complete until some years later, with the return of Nechemiah and the rebuilding of Yerushalayim.

Ge'ulah (Redemption): Old and New

AND THEN THE RA'AVAD ADDS A MOST noteworthy point, which may resolve the issue raised at the outset. So it will be, he states, with the future redemption. One day in the near future, Hashem will bring the *ge'ulah*. But this will also be a two-stage process. Even after the deliverance comes, the Jewish people will not immediately return to the Land. First, *Hashem will lead them through the desert,* as prophesied by Yechezkel: "And I will take you out from the nations and gather you from the lands into which you had been scattered... And I will bring you to the desert of the nations..." (*Yechezkel 20:34,35*). Rashi there identifies this "desert of the nations" as the desert through which B'nei Yisrael travelled for forty years.

R' Shternbuch explains the significance of this most remarkable statement: The future redemption from the current *galus* will be patterned, in many respects, after the redemption from Egypt. As the *passuk* states (*Michah 7:17*): "As in the days of your leaving Mitzrayim, I will show you wonders." Thus, when the final redemption arrives, the Jewish people will once again travel through the same desert-route as our forefathers did before entering the Land of Israel.

What emerges, then, is that the route outlined in this week's *parshah* is not merely insignificant historical data. Rather, every step of B'nei Yisrael's journey, through all the various locations, was actually laying the groundwork for the ultimate redemption – may we merit to see it soon!

This means that the entire section of B'nei Yisrael's travels in this week's *parshah* is a treasure trove of secrets, outlining the exact program of the final *ge'ulah*. Of course, the full extent of these hidden meanings will only be revealed in the future era. But the above idea provides us with a new perspective on this section of the Torah; reading through the list can engender hope and faith, with the realization that we are in effect reading the itinerary of our own redemption. And so, focusing on these hope-inspiring thoughts, we (literally) strike a triumphant note.

לזכר ולעילוי נשמת

רות בת משה ע"ה

SEFER DEVARIM

ספר דברים

לזכר ולעילוי נשמת
יוכבד בת יהודה ע"ה

DEVARIM

Re-examining the Churban: What Happened to the Beis Hamikdash?

WAS THE BEIS HAMIKDASH (HOLY TEMPLE) destroyed?

What a question! Of course it was. We have been, unfortunately, in exile for 2,000 years; there is currently no Beis Hamikdash at the Temple site; we yearn and pray daily for its rebuilding; and after all, isn't that what Tishah B'Av is all about? That certainly seems to be the plain meaning of the Mishnah, which states (*Ta'anis 4:6*):

בְּתִשְׁעָה בְּאָב נִגְזַר עַל אֲבוֹתֵינוּ שֶׁלֹּא יִכָּנְסוּ לָאָרֶץ, וְחָרַב הַבַּיִת בָּרִאשׁוֹנָה וּבַשְּׁנִיָּה...

"On the ninth of Av, it was decreed on our ancestors (during the episode of the spies) that they would not enter the Land, and both the first and second Temples were destroyed..."

KINDLY TAKE A MOMENT TO STUDY MISHNAS CHAYIM IN THE MERIT OF
YA'AKOV BEN CHAYIM *A"H*
A FELLOW JEW WHO PASSED AWAY WITH NO RELATIVES TO ARRANGE TORAH STUDY ON BEHALF OF HIS *NESHAMAH*

The central focus of the Tishah B'Av mourning is the *Churban* (destruction) of the Beis Hamikdash. So how can the question whether or not it was destroyed even be posed!?

In truth, as we shall see, the matter may not be all that simple. Of course, as *ma'aminim b'nei ma'aminim* (believers who are children of believers), we have perfect faith in what our Sages have said. The only question is, what exactly did they say? For while the intimation of the Mishnah seems clear, other statements from Chazal seem to point in a different direction.

CONSIDER, FOR EXAMPLE, THE FOLLOWING teaching of Chazal:

Your Eyes Can Deceive You
"R' Yitzchak said: At the time that the Beis Hamikdash was destroyed, Hakadosh Baruch Hu found that Avraham Avinu was standing in the Beis Hamikdash. He said to him: 'What is My beloved doing in My house?' (Avraham) answered: 'I have come on account of my children' " (Menachos 53b).

There are a number of points to be raised concerning this Gemara. First of all, if the Beis Hamikdash was in the middle of being destroyed, how could someone be standing in the midst of it, able to carry on a conversation? Furthermore, Avraham lived well before the time of the building of the first Beis Hamikdash! And if this takes place during Avraham's sojourn in the World of Truth, where all the righteous reside after their departure from this world, what, then, was he doing in the earthly Beis Hamikdash?

The *Otzros Hatorah* (*Tishah B'Av*) cites a very eye-opening passage from the Zohar (*parshas Pekudei*), which sheds much light on the issue. For it is here that Chazal seem to (explicitly) state that the Beis Hamikdash, in fact, was *not* destroyed at all:

"The Beis Hamikdash did not burn at all; nor did the hands of the nations damage it in any way. Rather, the malachim (angels) lifted it to the Heavens, with its interior completely intact. In its place, they constructed another (edifice) to fool the nations and deceive their

eyes. This is the edifice that was destroyed down below, but the real Beis Hamikdash was stored up Above!"

The remarkable statement of the Zohar, in fact, may even be reconcilable with the above-quoted Mishnah in Ta'anis. There is reason to mourn, of course, for the Beis Hamikdash has departed from its earthly site and the *Shechinah* (Divine Presence) with it. Apparently, however, the Beis Hamikdash was not destroyed; the Mishnah that states that it was destroyed may very well be referring to the replica that was constructed there by the *malachim*.

In any event, this accounts for the "placement" of Avraham Avinu within the confines of the Beis Hamikdash. The episode related by the Gemara could have taken place inside the Beis Hamikdash, even at the time of the *Churban*. It transpired within the *real* Beis Hamikdash, which had been hoisted on High to the realm of the Heavens, completely accessible to the *tzaddikim* residing there in the afterlife.

Back Again

IT SHOULD BE NOTED, HOWEVER, THAT IT APPEARS that this notion (of the real Beis Hamikdash simply being "placed in storage") was said specifically of the second Beis Hamikdash. Such emerges from a discourse of R' Yehonasan Eibshitz (*Ahavas Yehonasan, Haftarah for Shabbos Rosh Chodesh*) regarding the fate of the Second Temple.

R' Yehonasan was addressing some difficulties that arise regarding the *navi's* (prophet's) characterization of the two Temples: גָּדוֹל יִהְיֶה כְּבוֹד הַבַּיִת הַזֶּה הָאַחֲרוֹן מִן־הָרִאשׁוֹן אָמַר ד' – "The glory of this last Temple shall be greater than that of the first one, says Hashem" (*Chaggai 2:9*). The *navi* was comparing the First and Second Temples; why, then, did he refer to the Second Temple as the "last"? Isn't there supposed to be a Third Temple in the future? And how could it be described as "more glorious" than its predecessor? Chazal tell us that the Second Temple was missing certain key features that the First Temple had, such as the *Aron Hakodesh* (Holy Ark)!

In truth, R' Yehonasan explains, the Second Temple is appropriately termed the "last," for it *will* be the last; that is, it will actually return to serve as the Third Temple. In support of this idea, he quotes a *medrash* which – with some variation – resembles the aforementioned passage from the Zohar. The nations were tricked into thinking that they had burned down the second Beis Hamikdash. In truth, the structure had sunk into the ground – and it had done so in the manner of a seed. That is, in the future it will rejuvenate, sprouting forth from below to serve as the third Beis Hamikdash. This is also why it is considered to be more glorious than the First; as opposed to its predecessor, the second Beis Hamikdash has the advantage that it will return once again.

However, this is also not such a simple matter. While we know, yearn, and pray that the Beis Hamikdash will reappear soon, the manner in which this will take place is somewhat involved. From the above, it seems that it will sprout from the earth. But there are other intimations from Chazal, as well – a matter we will return to next week, *b'ezras Hashem.*

לזכר ולעילוי נשמות
אהרן בן אפרים זלמן הכהן ע״ה
טויבא חיה בת דוב ע״ה

VA'ESCHANAN

The Third Beis Hamikdash

(A significant portion of this article is based on the sefer Otzros Achris Hayamim, vol. I, ch. 9.)

WHEN A PERSON DEPARTS FROM THIS WORLD, Chazal tell us, he faces a Heavenly Tribunal that queries him about his lifetime activities. One of the six questions they ask is "*Tzipisa l'yeshuah* – Did you anxiously await the final redemption?" (*Shabbos 31a*).

There is a beautiful prevalent custom in Klal Yisrael that appears to serve, at least in part, as a fulfillment of this directive. It manifests itself in almost every major address, speech, or even Torah thought shared at a private celebration such as a *sheva berachos*. The practice entails adding a note of hope and comfort at the conclusion of the speech, invoking a prayer that we should merit to behold the rebuilding of the Beis Hamikdash (Holy Temple), "*Bimheirah v'yameinu* (speedily in our times), *amein*."

KINDLY TAKE A MOMENT TO STUDY MISHNAS CHAYIM IN THE MERIT OF
ZELDA BAS MOSHE A"H
A FELLOW JEW WHO PASSED AWAY WITH NO RELATIVES TO ARRANGE TORAH STUDY ON BEHALF OF HER *NESHAMAH*

This prayer mirrors the one we recite at the conclusion of Shemoneh Esreih, and appears, as well, in the Mishnah in Avos (5:20):

יְהִי רָצוֹן מִלְּפָנֶיךָ ד' אֱלֹקֵינוּ וֵאלֹקֵי אֲבוֹתֵינוּ, שֶׁיִּבָּנֶה בֵּית הַמִּקְדָּשׁ בִּמְהֵרָה בְיָמֵינוּ, וְתֵן חֶלְקֵנוּ בְּתוֹרָתֶךָ.

"May it be Your will, Hashem our G-d, and the G-d of our fathers, that the Beis Hamikdash will be rebuilt speedily in our days; and grant our portion in Your Torah."

From Below or Above?

THE ISSUE THAT ARISES IS THAT THESE WORDS, with which many are quite fluent, seem to contradict another familiar notion. Whether from popular songs or from the teachings from which the idea originated, we are used to picturing the re-emergence of the Beis Hamikdash in terms of a fully-constructed, ethereal edifice descending from on High.

There is real basis for this idea. Rashi writes the following in Sukkah (*41a, s.v. "Iy nami"*): מִקְדָּשׁ הֶעָתִיד שֶׁאָנוּ מְצַפִּין בָּנוּי וּמְשׁוּכְלָל הוּא יִגָּלֶה וְיָבֹא מִשָּׁמַיִם, שֶׁנֶּאֱמַר מִקְדָּשׁ ד' כּוֹנְנוּ יָדֶיךָ – "The future Beis Hamikdash for which we yearn is already fully constructed and ready; it will (simply) be revealed (to us) and will descend from the Heavens. As it states (*Shemos 15:17*): 'The Sanctuary, Hashem, established by Your hands.'" There is a work of Chazal known as Medrash Vayosha which, in discussing the events of the *Acharis Hayamim* (Final Days), states the same: וְהַהֵיכָל יוֹרִיד הקב"ה מִן הַשָּׁמַיִם כְּמוֹ שֶׁהֶרְאֵהוּ הקב"ה לְמֹשֶׁה – "Hashem will bring down the Sanctuary from the Heavens, in the manner that He had shown to Moshe."

As stated, however, there seem to be contradictory intimations. The position of Rashi (who is joined by numerous other Rishonim, such as Tosafos and the Ritva) – not to mention the clear statement of the Medrash Vayosha – is that the Third Beis Hamikdash is "pre-constructed," to be lowered by Hashem at the time of His choosing. But how does this square with the language of the oft-repeated prayer (mentioned also by Chazal themselves, as evidenced by the above citation from Avos) that states יְהִי רָצוֹן מִלְּפָנֶיךָ... שֶׁיִּבָּנֶה בֵּית הַמִּקְדָּשׁ – "May it be Your will... that the Temple shall be **built**"? If a completed structure was set to descend from on High, the seemingly more appropriate prayer would be שֶׁיִּגָּלֶה בֵּית הַמִּקְדָּשׁ – "that the Temple be **revealed**"! In its current form of שֶׁיִּבָּנֶה, the implication leans more to the position championed by the Rambam: namely, that it will be built by the hands of man. In his Introduction to Seder Zerai'm, the Rambam explains the purpose of Maseches Middos, which lists the dimensions of the various aspects of the Second Temple: "For when the Temple will be rebuilt speedily in our days, the building plan (as laid out in this *masechta*) must be followed." (In *Hilchos Melachim* [ch. 11], the Rambam writes that involvement in the construction of the Temple will fall under the purview of Mashiach himself.)

It All Fits Together

THE ARUCH LANEIR IN SUKKAH (*IBID.*) PRESENTS a novel and wondrous resolution. In fact, both are true – the Beis Hamikdash will be built by man and will also descend fully ready from Above. He explains by invoking another concept mentioned in Chazal: Namely, the two co-existing Temples – the Beis Hamikdash Shel Ma'alah (Temple of Above), residing (for now) in the Heavens, which corresponds to the earthly Temple, the Beis Hamikdash Shel Mattah (Temple of Below). What will take place in that glorious era is that the Third Temple will be rebuilt below, at which point Hashem will bring down the Beis Hamikdash Shel Ma'alah to dwell within the earthly Temple. Just as the physical human body contains within it a spiritual *neshamah* (soul), so, too, the ethereal Beis Hamikdash Shel Ma'alah will descend to earth to reside within and serve as the "*neshamah*" of the manmade Beis Hamikdash Shel Mattah.

This may be the meaning behind the *Nacheim* prayer inserted into the *minchah* Shemoneh Esreih of Tishah B'Av: כִּי אַתָּה ה' בָּאֵשׁ הִצַּתָּהּ, וּבָאֵשׁ אַתָּה עָתִיד לִבְנוֹתָהּ כָּאָמוּר וַאֲנִי אֶהְיֶה לָּהּ נְאֻם ה' חוֹמַת אֵשׁ סָבִיב – "For You, Hashem, have ignited a fire against (the Beis

Hamikdash), and with a fire You will rebuild it in the future; as is stated (*Zechariah 2:9*): 'And I will be for it a surrounding wall of fire...'" In a manner reminiscent of the above discussion we may ask: Will the future Beis Hamikdash be constructed from Heavenly fire or earthly material? Based on the Aruch Laneir, it would seem that both could be true; the "outer casing," which is the Beis Hamikdash Shel Mattah, will be manmade construction, while the inner "*neshamah*" of the Mikdash will be its spiritual essence sent down from on High.

We have taken this opportunity to at least nominally explore this issue, as it seems to be a topic in keeping with the *nechamah* (comforting) theme of Shabbos Nachamu. R' Shlomoh Brevda writes (*Yibaneh Hamikdash, p. 130*) that, in fact, this is the function of the series of seven "comforting" *haftarahs* recited during the post-Tishah B'Av weeks. By keeping the prophetic messages of the Final Redemption at the forefront of our focus, we are reminded of the essential (but all too often overlooked) fact that there is a *keitz*, an expiration, to our troubles and our *galus* (exile). While the precise details of the *ge'ulah* (redemption) are yet to be revealed in all of their fullness, we can at least take comfort that its imminent arrival will be wondrous indeed. As the *navi* (prophet) states: כִּימֵי צֵאתְךָ מֵאֶרֶץ מִצְרָיִם אַרְאֶנּוּ נִפְלָאוֹת - "As with the days of your exodus from the land of Egypt, I will show you wonders." May we merit to behold these wonders – and the rebuilding of the Beis Hamikdash – *bimheirah v'yameinu, Amein!*

לזכר ולעילוי נשמת
צבי הירש בן רחמיאל ע"ה
נסיה בת זאב ע"ה

EIKEV

The Hands of Moshe

OF COURSE, WE KNOW THAT MOSHE RABBEINU attained greatness. Concerning his quality of *anivus* (humility), the Torah attests: וְהָאִישׁ מֹשֶׁה עָנָיו מְאֹד מִכֹּל הָאָדָם אֲשֶׁר עַל־פְּנֵי הָאֲדָמָה – "And the man, Moshe, was more humble than any man that was on the face of the earth" (*Bamidbar 12:3*). A few *pessukim* later, Hashem declares of Moshe that he is "the most loyal of My entire household" and that he is the only *navi* (prophet) "with whom I speak mouth to mouth" (*v. 7,8*). And we are familiar with the fact that one of the thirteen principles of faith states that there never was, nor will there ever be, a *navi* equal to Moshe.

Furthermore, the Torah grants him a title that is perhaps one of the most complimentary with which a human being can be bestowed: "*Ish Ha'Elokim* – A man of G-d" (*Devarim 33:1*). Interestingly enough, the *medrash* (*Shocher Tov 90:5*) quantifies this description, asserting that this Divine-like quality of Moshe applied only to the top half of his body. What appears to be a manifestation of this idea plays itself out in this week's *parshah* in a most interesting way.

KINDLY TAKE A MOMENT TO STUDY MISHNAS CHAYIM IN THE MERIT OF
ROCHEL BAS YA'AKOV A"H
A FELLOW JEW WHO PASSED AWAY WITH NO RELATIVES TO ARRANGE TORAH STUDY ON BEHALF OF HER *NESHAMAH*

Endurance

A SIGNIFICANT PORTION OF *SEFER DEVARIM*, including this *parshah*, consists of Moshe's admonition to B'nei Yisrael. In the course of delivering this rebuke, Moshe recounts much of their past history, such as in this week's *parshah* when he recalls the episode of the Cheit Ha'eigel (Sin of the Golden Calf). In the midst of this narrative, however, he includes certain details that don't seem to fit with the admonishment theme. After relating how the original *luchos* (tablets containing the Ten Commandments) were destroyed on account of this idolatrous sin, Moshe tells of the fact that he was instructed to fashion an *aron* (ark) from wood to house the new set of *luchos*, which he proceeded to do: "And I turned and descended from the mountain, and I placed the *luchos* in the *aron* that I constructed; and there they resided" (*Devarim 10:5*). What place do these seemingly innocuous particulars have in the context of the national admonition?

R' Moshe Feinstein (*Darash Moshe*) explains how this notion is also a fitting part of the rebuke. The fact that the *luchos* were to be placed in an *aron* was itself a byproduct of the Cheit Ha'eigel – for that was not the original plan. Thus, by mentioning that this second set of *luchos* was to be hidden from view and housed in an *aron*, Moshe was underscoring the negative ramifications of their actions and the exalted opportunity they had lost.

What had been the original plan? If the first *luchos* were not to be stored in an *aron*, where would they be placed? R' Moshe asserts that, were it not for the sin, *Moshe Rabbeinu himself would have served as the aron*. Earlier in the *parshah*, Moshe Rabbeinu describes his original descent from the mountain bearing the first set of *luchos*: "And the two Luchos of the Covenant were upon my two hands" (*ibid. 9:15*). This was their intended destination – i.e., they would constantly be resting on Moshe's hands. This is no small feat, especially considering the fact that the *luchos* weighed somewhere in the neighborhood of half a ton (according to the Yerushalmi [*Ta'anis 4:5*], they weighed the equivalent of forty *se'ahs* worth of water). Unfortunately, due to the Cheit Ha'eigel, this arrangement was not to be; instead of remaining constantly in full view, displayed on Moshe's arms, the *luchos* were essentially hidden from view in the confines of an *aron*. But the fact that Moshe would have been able to bear such a load, and was considered to possess significant sanctity to serve as an *aron kodesh*, seems to be a testament to the superhuman, "G-dly" quality of even his physical body (at least the upper half).

Powered by Kavannah

THIS IS ACTUALLY NOT THE FIRST TIME MOSHE'S arms were singled out in connection with some extra-natural phenomenon. Another example took place during the war with Amalek. The Torah records how the outcome of the war seemed to follow the positioning of Moshe's arms. As the *passuk* states: וְהָיָה כַּאֲשֶׁר יָרִים מֹשֶׁה יָדוֹ וְגָבַר יִשְׂרָאֵל וְכַאֲשֶׁר יָנִיחַ יָדוֹ וְגָבַר עֲמָלֵק – "And it was, when Moshe would lift his hand, Yisrael would prevail; and when he would lay down his hand, Amalek would prevail" (*Shemos* 17:11). There is an obvious question that arises with regard to this arrangement. If Yisrael's success in the battle depended on the uplifting of Moshe's hands – then why would he lay them down? Was it simply that he was too tired?

Insight into this issue can be gleaned by examining the well-known teaching of Chazal that addresses the other central point: Was the war really being controlled by Moshe's hands? The Mishnah states (*Rosh Hashanah* 3:8):

> וְכִי יָדָיו שֶׁל מֹשֶׁה עוֹשׂוֹת מִלְחָמָה אוֹ שׁוֹבְרוֹת מִלְחָמָה. אֶלָּא לוֹמַר לָךְ, כָּל זְמַן שֶׁהָיוּ יִשְׂרָאֵל מִסְתַּכְּלִים כְּלַפֵּי מַעְלָה וּמְשַׁעְבְּדִין אֶת לִבָּם לַאֲבִיהֶם שֶׁבַּשָּׁמַיִם הָיוּ מִתְגַּבְּרִים. וְאִם לָאו, הָיוּ נוֹפְלִין.

> "Could the hands of Moshe really make or break a war? Rather, (the verse) is telling you: As long as Yisrael would gaze Heavenward and subjugate their hearts to their Father in Heaven, they would prevail. If not, they would falter."

In his comments on this Mishnah, the Maharsha makes an important and intriguing point. What, to be precise, is the Mishnah telling us? That it wasn't Moshe's hands after all that were controlling the war, but rather Yisrael's purity of heart and subservience to Hashem? So what role, exactly, did Moshe's hands play in the battle?

The Maharsha clarifies the Mishnah's intent. It was not that Moshe's hands determined the outcome of the war, but, to an extent, it was the other way around. The outcome was determined by the directing Heavenward of Yisrael's heart. *And it was this that had a direct effect on Moshe's hands.* The uplifting of Moshe's hands, as one does when beseeching the Almighty, symbolized the directing of their hearts to Him. And when Yisrael would in fact look Heavenward, Moshe's hands would automatically be raised. However, when the subservience of their hearts to Hashem would be interrupted, the force holding up Moshe's hands would fall.

In effect, then, Moshe's hands took on the role of a "weather vane" of sorts. Not that it showed which way the wind was blowing, but it indicated in which direction the hearts of Yisrael were directed.

לזכר ולעילוי נשמת
יואלת בת אברהם חנא ע"ה

RE'EH

No Retirement

A CERTAIN INDIVIDUAL WHO SERVED AS AN AGENT (in a wood-selling business) for the venerated Maharsham passed away. While he had faithfully discharged his employment duties, he was much more delinquent in his approach to Torah and *mitzvos*. He appeared numerous times in a dream to the Maharsham; the latter would consistently engage in mitzvah acts (e.g., giving *tzedakah*, learning *mishnayos*) on behalf of his soul. These had their salutary effect; he was offered certain reprieves from retribution and was eventually granted access to eternal reward. At that point, the late agent appeared to the Maharsham to express his gratitude and informed him that he would no longer be "visiting." On this final visit, the Maharsham asked if he could relate the details of his Heavenly station. The man replied that while these matters are generally not revealed to the living, he could share certain aspects for the sake of such a great sage. And this is what he said (as recorded by the Maharsham's son):

> "... In the Upper World, there are yeshivos, rooms, and (study) groups – just as in This World. Each group

---

KINDLY TAKE A MOMENT TO STUDY MISHNAS CHAYIM IN THE MERIT OF
SHIMON BEN MENASHE A"H
A FELLOW JEW WHO PASSED AWAY WITH NO RELATIVES TO ARRANGE TORAH STUDY ON BEHALF OF HIS *NESHAMAH*

is stationed in its designated room. The exalted holy ones... study Kabbalah; the great halachic experts... learn (the Torah of the) poskim (halachic decisors); and so there is for Gemara, Mishnah and Tanach... Each group learns in its designated room and derives pleasure from the radiance of the Shechinah (Divine Presence). It is impossible to describe the extent of the delight these study groups enjoy.

"One who neglected to learn any Torah in This World... but nevertheless was (eventually) granted access to eternal reward stands outside and hears the sound of the learners emanating through the windows. The place where one stands depends on the level of merit he accrued through whatever he prepared in This World. If one were to attempt to describe, in writing, the colossal delight enjoyed... by merely listening to those learning and gazing upon their torch-like countenance, with the Shechinah literally resting among them – no parchment could possibly offer sufficient space...

"I myself did not merit... to view this, for not everyone merits to behold how the holy ones and the Torah scholars – for whom Torah study was their occupation in This World – are taught Torah, some by Hashem Himself, some by Eliyahu Hanavi, each one according to what he prepared while still in This World. Nevertheless, I also enjoy intense spiritual delight, to which all silver, gold and worldly pleasures cannot measure up... even to just one moment of simply hearing the learning in progress, without being able to see...

"More than this, I have neither the time nor authorization to reveal to you" (Sefer L'iluy Neshamah, pp. 125-127).

This account underscores a wondrous contingency that exists regarding the mitzvah of Talmud Torah (Torah study). That is, this mitzvah is distinct from all others in that the endeavor continues even after one departs from This World. (It should be noted, as well, that the above represents only the proverbial tip of the iceberg; particularly in the works of Chazal [e.g., Maseches Gan Eden], the situation of Torah study in Gan Eden is described in considerable length. In this particular forum, however, "the parchment does not provide sufficient space...").

This notion can shed much light on another aspect of the uniqueness of this mitzvah, one highlighted in this week's *parshah*.

Timely Payment

A CONTRADICTION SEEMS TO EMERGE FROM THE beginning of this week's *parshah*, which states: רְאֵה אָנֹכִי נֹתֵן לִפְנֵיכֶם הַיּוֹם בְּרָכָה וּקְלָלָה, אֶת־הַבְּרָכָה אֲשֶׁר תִּשְׁמְעוּ אֶל־מִצְוֹת ד' – "See that I have placed before you this day a blessing and a curse; the blessing (comes if) you listen to the *mitzvos* of Hashem" (*Devarim 11:26,27*). The implication is that the blessing and reward will arrive "*hayom* – today," even in This World. How does this square with Chazal's statement (*Kiddushin 39b*) that שְׂכַר מִצְוָה בְּהַאי עָלְמָא לֵיכָּא – "Reward for a mitzvah is not granted in This World (but only in the Next)"? The issue may be resolved by the comments of the Ba'al Haturim. He understands the *passuk* as referring to the mitzvah of Torah study, as alluded to in the final letters of the words אֶת־הַבְּרָכָה אֲשֶׁר תִּשְׁמְעוּ, which, when rearranged, form the word תּוֹרָה. In other words, שְׂכַר מִצְוָה בְּהַאי עָלְמָא לֵיכָּא is the general rule; the mitzvah of Torah study is the exception.

The outstanding question, however, is why? What is it about Torah study that enables one to receive some reward even during one's lifetime?

The Ohr Chadash (*Kiddushin 39b*) presents a resolution, based on the laws governing wages. The Torah mandates that a hired worker must be paid "on time," the parameters of which are delineated in the Mishnah (*Bava Metzia 9:11*):

שְׂכִיר יוֹם גּוֹבֶה כָּל הַלַּיְלָה, שְׂכִיר לַיְלָה גּוֹבֶה כָּל הַיּוֹם.

"A day laborer may be paid anytime during the night; a night laborer, by day."

The Gemara (*ibid. 110b*) wonders why we don't say the reverse; perhaps a day laborer must be paid while it is yet day, and the night laborer before the night is over? The Gemara answers that a foundational principle is at work here: שְׂכִירוּת אֵינָהּ מִשְׁתַּלֶּמֶת אֶלָּא בַּסּוֹף – The obligation on the employer to pay the wages begins only upon the *completion* of the work period. Regarding a day laborer, then, the employer need not even contemplate paying wages until the night begins – and then he has the remainder of the night to pay. The opposite holds true with a night worker.

The same principle can be applied to the reward (*s'char*) for *mitzvos*. Why is it that *s'char* is not granted in This World? The reason, explains the Ohr Chadash, is the same. The obligation to pay wages only begins at the end of the work period. As it relates to *mitzvos*, the "work period" is not over so long as a person is still alive; it is only when he departs from This World that the time to collect his "wages" arrives.

And this is why Talmud Torah is an exception. Because, as we have seen above, *the "work-period" for Torah study never ends.* The entirety of the "payment" for this mitzvah cannot be delayed until one departs from This World because even then the task is not finished. Therefore, this dispensation was allowed with regard to the mitzvah of Torah study. For this mitzvah, the blessing and *s'char* may be bestowed even "*hayom*" – in This World.

לזכר ולעילוי נשמת
זאב וואלף לייב בן צבי הערש מרדכי ע"ה

SHOFTIM

Men and Trees

A condensed digest of various interpretations to a very intriguing passuk

THERE IS A PARTICULAR *PASSUK* IN THIS WEEK'S *parshah*, set in the context of the laws governing battle, whose meaning seems quite elusive. Obtaining a simple rendering of this verse is somewhat of a challenge, as evidenced by the concerted efforts on the part of a number of commentaries in arriving at its interpretation. Rashi on the very first *passuk* in the Torah makes the following statement: אֵין הַמִּקְרָא הַזֶּה אוֹמֵר אֶלָּא דּוֹרְשֵׁנִי – "This verse virtually demands explanation!" It would seem that such a sentiment would be applicable in this case, as well. To illustrate, we will simply present the *passuk* here, followed by a literal translation. The perplexities should be self-evident.

כִּי־תָצוּר אֶל־עִיר... לֹא־תַשְׁחִית אֶת־עֵצָהּ... כִּי מִמֶּנּוּ תֹאכֵל וְאֹתוֹ לֹא תִכְרֹת כִּי הָאָדָם עֵץ הַשָּׂדֶה לָבֹא מִפָּנֶיךָ בַּמָּצוֹר.

KINDLY TAKE A MOMENT TO STUDY MISHNAS CHAYIM IN THE MERIT OF
YA'AKOV BEN CHAYIM A"H
A FELLOW JEW WHO PASSED AWAY WITH NO RELATIVES TO ARRANGE TORAH STUDY ON BEHALF OF HIS *NESHAMAH*

"When you lay siege against a city... do not destroy its trees... for from them shall you eat, and you shall not cut it down, **for a man is a tree of the field to come from before you into the siege**" (*Devarim 20:19*).

What does that mean?

To list all of the various interpretations proffered by the commentators would be well beyond the scope of this forum; as such, we will have to suffice by presenting a limited selection.

Intimidation and Provocation

THERE DOES SEEM TO BE AN IMPLIED EQUATION OF men and trees – something which, in itself, requires elucidation. Some commentators do, in fact, understand the *passuk* in this manner. What is clear is that the Torah is warning against the destruction of trees, even in the course of battle. Rashi interprets the verse as presenting a rhetorical question: What purpose is there in cutting down the trees? Is a tree like a person, whose elimination would serve a practical purpose in war? If an unfortunate is seized on the outside of a besieged city, his life is basically forfeit; the enemy will dispatch him in order to reinforce the siege. His death serves to "convince" the city's inhabitants to remain inside the besieged city, despite the deprivations of thirst and hunger that result from the siege. However, a tree that is located outside the city is a different matter; its destruction will not serve this same purpose. This is what the *passuk* is conveying: "... Do not cut it down, for is a tree like a person (that its elimination will cause the onlookers) to retreat from before you into the besieged city?" (*cf. Mizrachi*).

Tosafos (*Da'as Zekeinim MiBa'alei HaTosafos*) takes a completely different approach than Rashi. Another somewhat complex aspect of this *passuk* is the term "*ki*," which Chazal tell us (*Gittin 90a*) could have any one of four meanings. Rashi apparently adopted the definition of "perhaps" – "Perhaps a tree is like a man?" – in presenting the rhetorical approach. Tosafos chooses the definition of "rather/only" and render the *passuk* not in question form, but as a qualifier. They understand that the directive to avoid cutting down trees does not apply when there is a pressing need. For example, if there are thick woods in proximity to the besieged city in which the inhabitants may hide (and even attempt to infiltrate the camp of the besieging army), these trees may be cleared away. The *passuk*, then, would read as follows: "Do not cut it down *unless* people (may utilize) the trees to enter within your besieging camp."

The Netziv (*Ha'amek Davar*) provides a novel interpretation based on a strategic military tactic. The purpose of a siege, obviously, is the eventual conquest of the city – preferably sooner rather than later. A besieging army may attempt to speed up the city's downfall by sending in provocateurs. These individuals are disguised and attempt to blend in with the besieged inhabitants. However, they cleverly instigate strife amongst the citizens. Due to the deterioration of the internal situation and the ensuing confusion, the opportunity arises to throw open the gates to admit the imposters' true brothers-in-arms.

Now, when the army enters the city to lay it to waste, will they kill these agents with the other inhabitants? Of course not! They are on the same side, and they greatly aided the warriors. This, the Netziv explains, is the message of the *passuk*. Adopting the definition of "because," he interprets the verse as prohibiting the destruction of the fruit trees on account of the help they afford the besieging army, providing them with sustenance. "Do not cut it down because a tree is like the people who infiltrate the besieged city on your behalf (and just as you would not kill those assistants, do not kill your arboreal helpers, either).

If a Tree Were to Fall Where No One Could Hear it...

INTERESTINGLY, THE TZROR HAMOR SEEMS TO TAKE the comparison of men to trees literally – to an extent. He cites the *medrash* (*Pirkei D'R'Eliezer*, ch. 34), which states: "When a fruit-bearing tree is cut down, it emits a scream that reverberates from one end of the world to the other – but alas, it is not heard." The Tzror

Hamor explains that this is so because, just like a person, a tree also has an aspect of a soul that has feeling.

Another shared facet of both trees and man is the production of "*peiros*" (fruit). Consider the statement of the familiar Mishnah, incorporated into our daily prayers (*Peah 1:1*):

> אֵלּוּ דְבָרִים שֶׁאָדָם אוֹכֵל פֵּרוֹתֵיהֶן בָּעוֹלָם הַזֶּה וְהַקֶּרֶן קַיֶּמֶת לוֹ לָעוֹלָם הַבָּא...

> "These are the things that one eats from their 'fruit' in This World, yet the principal remains (to be enjoyed) in the World to Come..."

Thus we see that the real fruits of one's labor are his good deeds. In any event, the Tzror Hamor understands that a man is likened to a tree principally in these two ways. There are differences also, of course. Most significantly, a man has intelligence and ability to make choices and flee from danger, while a tree does not. Thus, he interprets the *passuk* as relating both the similarities and differences between man and tree, rendering it as follows: "Do not cut it down, for a man is like a tree (in that both can feel and both produce fruit. However, a tree is different and at a disadvantage, in that) it cannot escape from before your onslaught into the city. (Therefore, it is not appropriate to cut it down.)"

לזכר ולעילוי נשמת

אליהו בן אברהם משה ע"ה

KI SEITZEI

A Joyous Breakdown

HAVE YOU EVER HAD THE EXPERIENCE OF BEING stuck in an hours-long traffic jam? Or breaking down, waiting in your car by the side of the rode until some form of assistance (hopefully) arrives? Imagine how it must have been a century or so ago with horse-drawn carriages; if something should happen, there's not even an option of taking out a cellphone and having some tow-truck drive over to address the situation.

But just such a thing occurred to the saintly R' Nosson Adler, *rebbi* of the Chasam Sofer. It was no less than midwinter, in the midst of a snow-covered landscape, when the wagon that was carrying the *rebbi* and his disciple ground to a halt. Instead of the "engine" conking out, it was one of the two horses that chose this most inopportune time and place to breathe its last. Far from any trace of civilization, the travelers were faced with the prospect of many, many hours in the cold until some form of replacement would appear.

R' Nosson Adler reacted by breaking out in joyous dancing. Why? As we shall see, the cause is rooted in this week's *parshah*.

Kindly take a moment to study Mishnas Chayim in the merit of
Aharon Reuven *ben* Avrohom *a"h*
a fellow Jew who passed away with no relatives to arrange Torah study on behalf of his *neshamah*

Opportunity Knocks

ONE OF THE *MITZVOS* DELINEATED IN THE *PARSHAH* is the prohibition against plowing with a combination of animals. As the *passuk* states: לֹא תַחֲרֹשׁ בְּשׁוֹר וּבַחֲמֹר יַחְדָּו – "Do not plow with an ox and donkey together" (*Devarim 22:10*). Actually, the commentators clarify that the prohibition is not limited to the items mentioned in the *passuk*, which were selected more by way of example. Thus, one violates the prohibition by using a combination other than an ox and a donkey. Furthermore, it is not only plowing together that is forbidden, but other forms of joint pulling are prohibited as well. The Mishnah (*Kilayim 8:2,3*) demonstrates how far-reaching the prohibition can be:

אֲסוּרִין לַחֲרֹשׁ וְלִמְשֹׁךְ וּלְהַנְהִיג... וְהַיּוֹשֵׁב בַּקָּרוֹן סוֹפֵג אֶת הָאַרְבָּעִים.

> "It is forbidden to (have a combination) plow, bear (a load or wagon), or be led together... (Even) one who (merely) sits in a wagon (drawn by a forbidden combination) incurs the penalty of forty lashes (as with any standard prohibition)."

Against this backdrop we can return to R' Nosson Adler's encounter. He sat waiting with his *talmid*, the Chasam Sofer, as the wagoner ventured to the nearest village to obtain a replacement horse. As this entailed a sizeable distance, the pair had to endure the elements for quite some time until they finally recognized the figure of the driver with another animal in tow. But as he drew nearer, R' Nosson discerned that it wasn't a horse... but a donkey instead.

When R' Nosson beheld this development, he became ecstatic. The Chasam Sofer questioned the reason for his joy, and R' Nosson explained: "I spend most of my days in my hometown, closeted in study. I never dreamed that I would have a chance to fulfill the dictum of 'Do not plow with an ox and donkey together.' And yet today, that's exactly what happened. When I saw the wagoner had brought a donkey to join with the horse, I realized right away that we would have an even longer wait, as the donkey will have to be sent back in exchange for a proper horse. An opportunity to fulfill this mitzvah is surely a cause for celebration!"

A Forgotten Mitzvah

WHAT IS SOMEWHAT HUMBLING ABOUT A STORY OF this nature is the contrast it highlights between some of our prevalent attitudes and those of the more elevated spirits. We may have reacted with bitterness at the prospect of having to wait even longer because of the driver's error; by contrast, R' Nosson literally broke out in dancing.

Interestingly enough, Chazal relate a similar incident – one also involving a mitzvah in this week's *parshah*. The mitzvah of *shikchah* obligates a farmer who realizes that he forgot a bundle in the field to refrain from retrieving it; it is to be left, instead, for the poor to come and take possession.

Imagine if you or I were faced with such a situation – what would be the "gut-reaction"? It might not be such a happy experience. "Oh, no!" we might say. "How could I forget? Well, there goes a whole bundle down the drain."

But the Tosefta (*Pe'ah 3:13*) tells of a much different reaction:

> "It once happened that a certain pious individual forgot his sheaf in the midst of his field. (Upon realizing his mistake), he remarked to his son: 'Go, and sacrifice on my behalf one bull as a burnt-offering and one bull as a peace-offering.' (His son) said to him: 'Father, what have you seen to rejoice over this particular mitzvah more than any of the mitzvos of the Torah?' (The father) said to him: 'Regarding any other mitzvah of the Torah, Hashem provides us the opportunity to fulfill them from our own knowledge. But this mitzvah (of shikchah) can only come about if it is not from our knowledge; for if Hashem would not will it, the opportunity to perform it would never come to our hands.'"

The pious man's attitude is most instructive. How many people would be only too thrilled if it they never had the opportunity to part with their possessions due to a lapse in awareness? On the contrary; if it did happen that they forgot, they might well be upset to learn about the forgotten sheaf that they will now have to forego. But the pious feel differently; the one featured above would have been upset *not* to have had the "fortune" to forget. When he actually did, he was elated; so grateful was he for the chance to fulfill this mitzvah and part with his possessions that he hastened to give away even more, in the form of sacrifices to Hashem.

לזכר ולעילוי נשמת
שרה בת חיים ע״ה

KI SAVO

Fuel for Flight

FEEDING THE BIRDS IS A VERY POPULAR ACTIVITY IN many yards across the globe. More than an opportunity to see these feathery creatures up close and "connect with nature," it appears from the *sefarim* (sacred works) that significant spiritual ramifications emanate from this practice.

Emulation
ONE AREA IN WHICH THIS IDEA SURFACES IS IN connection with a mitzvah in this week's *parshah*, which commands us: וְהָלַכְתָּ בִּדְרָכָיו – "And you shall walk in His ways" (*Devarim 28:9*). The *Sefer Hachinuch* (§611) lists this directive as a *mitzvas aseih* (positive commandment) to emulate the ways of Hashem and cultivate those attributes and practices with which He is associated. As Chazal state: "Just as Hashem is known as 'Merciful,' so should you be merciful..." (*Sifri, Parshas Eikev*); "Hashem visits the sick... so should you visit the sick..." (*Sotah 14a*).

The *mussar* classic *Tomar Devorah*, in its opening chapter, delineates the numerous merciful attributes of Hashem that one

---

KINDLY TAKE A MOMENT TO STUDY MISHNAS CHAYIM IN THE MERIT OF
SHMUEL BEN YA'AKOV A"H
A FELLOW JEW WHO PASSED AWAY WITH NO RELATIVES TO ARRANGE TORAH STUDY ON BEHALF OF HIS *NESHAMAH*

should develop in order to emulate His ways. At the close of this chapter, he adds that a person who conducts himself in this manner will reap much benefit and Celestial assistance. For if a person below adheres to such conduct, there will be a reciprocal reaction from Heaven, such that one who acts mercifully will merit an outpouring from Above of the corresponding Divine attribute.

One relatively simple way to achieve this is through the practice mentioned at the outset. The *Sefer Chareidim* (*14:1*) states that feeding Hashem's needy creatures is subsumed within this mitzvah of "*V'halachta bidrachav.*" Such behavior is in consonance with that conduct of Hashem described in the *Ashrei* prayer: טוֹב ד' לַכֹּל וְרַחֲמָיו עַל־כָּל־מַעֲשָׂיו – "Hashem is good to all, and His mercies extend to all of His creations" (*Tehillim 145:9*). Thus, the *Shulchan Hatahor* (*ch. 2*) relates that it is a customary practice of the pious to put out food for the birds during times of extreme cold and that doing so arouses the attribute of Divine mercy upon the world.

In certain noteworthy passages, Chazal likewise refer to this aspect of Hashem as the Benevolent Provider of the needs of all of His creatures – from the most majestic and large to the most insignificant. As the Gemara states: יוֹשֵׁב הקב"ה וְזָן מִקַּרְנֵי רְאֵמִים וְעַד בֵּיצֵי כִינִים – "Hashem sits and provides sustenance to (all; from) the horned *re'eimim* (certain herbivores of considerable size) down to lice-hatchlings" (*Avodah Zarah 3b*).

Likewise, special reference is made to the kindness Hashem demonstrates toward birds of the nest. This is done in the context of considering the suitability of certain prayer-formulations; as the Mishnah states (*Berachos 5:3*):

הָאוֹמֵר עַל קַן צִפּוֹר יַגִּיעוּ רַחֲמֶיךָ... מְשַׁתְּקִין אוֹתוֹ.

"One who says, 'Your mercy extends to a bird's nest,' is silenced."

The commentators point out that it is not the actual substance of this declaration that is objectionable, but rather, the implication as it relates to the mitzvah of *shilu'ach hakan* (sending away the mother bird from the nest before taking the eggs [*Devarim*

22:6,7]). The individual mouthing this praise is insinuating that this is the primary reason we should follow the mitzvah: *because it is merciful*. This is a tremendous error, one which Chazal state must be vehemently corrected; we follow the *mitzvos* because the King has so commanded, whether we understand their underlying reasons or not. But it is definitely true that Hashem's mercy is displayed through this mitzvah, as Chazal themselves state: "Hashem is filled with compassion upon the birds. From where do we know this? As it states (*ibid.*): 'When you encounter a bird's nest...'" (*Devarim Rabbah 6:1; cf. Peirush Maharzu*).

Salvation through Bird-Feeding

FURTHERMORE, NEGLECTING THE NEEDS OF BIRDS in one's care and causing them to suffer deprivation can result in severe consequences. The *Sefer Chareidim* (*ibid.*) relates a frightening account in this regard, involving the saintly Arizal. This venerable sage had so refined his character that his spiritual senses were exceedingly sharp; he could discern a person's spiritual standing by merely looking at him. So it happened that he once peered at the face of a certain Torah scholar and informed him that he could tell from his face that he had violated the prohibition against causing pain to animals (*tza'ar ba'alei chayim*).

A conscientious fellow, the scholar was perturbed and perplexed. He was not a vicious person. When did he ever cause harm to animals? Further examination uncovered the fact that his wife, who cared for the chickens, had been somewhat negligent in providing the birds' morning fare. Instead of placing food before them, she merely allowed them to wander the courtyard to fend for themselves, sufficing with whatever morsels they happened to come upon.

After this discovery, the scholar advised his wife to prepare the proper chicken-victuals each morning and place them in the chickens' yard. She did so, and the next time the man appeared before the Arizal, the sage told him: "I see that the iniquity has been erased."

R' Yitzchak Zilberstein relates a similar incident reported to R' Chaim Kanievsky. A couple had been childless for a while, and the husband would visit R' Chaim for advice and blessings.

One day, the man appeared before R' Chaim with glad tidings that they had been blessed with a child. He told R' Chaim what had transpired.

Some concerned friends of his had shown him *sefarim* citing the mistreatment of animals as a reason why one might be prevented from childbearing. The couple wondered how this could be applicable to them – until they recalled something. For some time, their porch had been "infested" by the local pigeons, who apparently found this particular location to be the perfect spot to congregate. The owners then poured tar around the area, which chased away the "pests."

"After learning that such behavior could be responsible for our situation," the man continued, "we decided to engage in a form of penance. I scattered breadcrumbs on the porch, and soon enough, the birds came back. Shortly after that, we were blessed with a child" (*Tuvcha Yabi'u, Parshas Ki Savo*).

לזכר ולעילוי נשמות
ר' חיים בן הרב יעקב בן ציון ע״ה
רחל בת מאיר ע״ה

NITZAVIM

Take Up Your Weapons

(The following analysis of the principal Rosh Hashanah services is based in large part on an exposition by R' Yeruchem Olshin in Yerach L'mo'adim, Yamim Nora'im I, ma'amar 47, §1-4.)

IN CERTAIN RESPECTS, ROSH HASHANAH MAY SEEM like a confusing time. Such might be the impression one gets from a cursory glance at the day's practices.

Combination Package

OF COURSE, AS WE KNOW, ROSH HASHANAH IS A solemn and serious time, as the world stands in judgment before Hashem over the most significant issues of life and death. As R' Yisrael Salanter writes (*Ohr Yisrael §7*): "A person – and all who rely on him – are in a *sakanah gedolah* (grave danger) during this time of judgment." As Hakadosh Baruch Hu examines one's deeds and determines his fate, a primary method for addressing this *sakanah* is through the endeavor of *teshuvah* (repentance) to rectify one's "record." The mitzvah of blowing the shofar fits well with this notion, as the Rambam famously remarks that

---

KINDLY TAKE A MOMENT TO STUDY MISHNAS CHAYIM IN THE MERIT OF
REUVEN BEN AVROHOM A"H
A FELLOW JEW WHO PASSED AWAY WITH NO RELATIVES TO ARRANGE TORAH STUDY ON BEHALF OF HIS NESHAMAH

the message and purpose of the shofar is to arouse us to repent (*Hilchos Teshuvah 3:4*).

One would have imagined, then, that the bulk of the day would be dedicated to involvement in *teshuvah*. Certainly it is a major component of the day, and the more thoroughly one applies himself to this task, the better. Yet, when we look at the overall picture, it seems that most of our time and energy on this day is spent immersed in prayer. Not only that, but the theme of *teshuvah* doesn't even seem to figure so prominently in the service. Of course it is mentioned, as is the notion that Hashem sits in judgment. But insofar as the liturgy is concerned, these seem to receive relatively sporadic attention. It almost seems as if the theme of "Kingship" is as central (if not more so) to the day as *teshuvah* or shofar.

The dual nature of the day's service is further reflected in the order of the *Mussaf* service, as delineated in the Mishnah (*Rosh Hashanah 4:5*):

אוֹמֵר אָבוֹת וּגְבוּרוֹת וּקְדֻשַּׁת הַשֵּׁם, וְכוֹלֵל מַלְכֻיּוֹת עִם קְדֻשַּׁת הַיּוֹם, וְתוֹקֵעַ. זִכְרוֹנוֹת, וְתוֹקֵעַ. שׁוֹפָרוֹת, וְתוֹקֵעַ. וְאוֹמֵר עֲבוֹדָה וְהוֹדָאָה וּבִרְכַּת כֹּהֲנִים.

"One recites Avos, Gevuros, and Kedushas Hashem (the first three blessings of any Shemoneh Esreih) and includes (the blessing of) Malchiyos ("Kingship") with Kedushas Hashem, and the shofar is blown. (He then recites the blessing of) Zichronos ("Remembrances"), and the shofar is blown, (followed by the recital of the blessing of) Shofaros, and the shofar is blown. He (then) recites Avodah, Hoda'ah, and the Priestly Blessing (including Sim Shalom, i.e., he recites the final three blessings of any Shemoneh Esreih)."

Here we see some type of interplay between these seemingly disparate entities. What, indeed, is the relationship between shofar blowing and the recital of *Malchiyos, Zichronos,* and *Shofros*?

The Netziv clarifies this issue, as well as the others raised above. He does so by informing us that a lot more transpires on Rosh Hashanah than we might realize.

The Nations Conspire

IN A LANDMARK PIECE IN *HARCHEIV DAVAR* (*VAYIKRA 23:24*), the Netziv explains that there are actually *two* judgments that take place on this day. One involves the individual judgment every person undergoes, in which his affairs for the coming year are determined. But then there is a second matter of contention that is addressed on this day, affecting the Jewish nation as a whole. This occurs in the Upper realms, wherein the Celestial representatives of all the nations below coalesce as a group of litigants. They appear before Hashem and attempt to annul the special relationship between Him and Yisrael. R' Shlomoh Kluger (*Chachmas Shlomoh 581:64*) states similarly, explaining that they take aim at the Jews' status as the "Chosen People," urging the Almighty to renege on His choice. This, then, is the essence of this second judgment: will Yisrael remain Hashem's "Chosen People"?

As stated previously, one of the most basic methods of addressing the first judgment – affecting the lives of individuals – is through heartfelt *teshuvah*. How is this second peril addressed? The Netziv derives the answer from a most illuminating passage in the Yerushalmi. When the leader of the services approaches the lectern, how should he be encouraged? Should we tell him, "Do a great job?" "*Daven* well?" These may seem to be sensible options, but the Yerushalmi (*Berachos ch. 5*) states differently. Apparently, the officiator of the prayers is told to prepare for war.

The Netziv understands this as a reference to the Celestial battle waged by the angelic representatives of the nations against Yisrael. For it is prayer that is the most effective weapon in this conflict, specifically the verbal coronation of Hashem through the recital of *Malchiyos*, *Zichronos*, and *Shofros*. This is why we find "Kingship" playing such a prominent role in the order of the day. At this desperate time, this is the optimal way to ensure that Hashem will not be swayed by these Celestial accusers. In effect, we are pleading with Him to retain us as His people, as we proclaim that He is our King.

This notion also sheds much light on the role of the shofar in the day's service. True, the shofar assists in the effort for *teshuvah*, aiding a Jew to be granted a favorable judgment in his personal accounting. But this applies only to the blowing of the shofar that takes place *before Mussaf*, when it stands on its own. The shofar-blowing that is integrated into the *Mussaf* service, explains the Netziv, serves a different function. He likens it to the use of the *chatzotzros* (trumpets) that would be sounded at a time of battle (*Bamidbar 10:9*). Here, the purpose was to aid the battle effort, primarily by arousing the people to pray for success. Similarly, the shofar is sounded during *Mussaf* – which itself is a time of battle. Thus, as we recite the *Malchiyos, Zichoronos,* and *Shofros,* we do battle with the Celestial representatives who seek our dissolution.

The above grants us much insight into the day's service. In addition to the essential acts of shofar blowing and *teshuvah*, we engage extensively in *tefillah*. This is our principal weapon in our battle against these pernicious forces: proclaiming His Kingship and pleading that we remain His people. This will occur, as we recite: כִּי תַעֲבִיר מֶמְשֶׁלֶת זָדוֹן מִן הָאָרֶץ – "When You shall remove the dominion of evil from the earth."

This prayer, which we also recite on Yom Kippur, contains another layer of meaning particularly pertinent to the times in which we live. We will explore this next week, *b'ezras Hashem*.

לזכר ולעילוי נשמת
אברהם בן דוד ע"ה

VAYEILECH

The Final Surge

IN ONE OF THE DRAMATIC PASSAGES FROM THE *Yamim Nora'im* liturgy, we recite: כִּי תַעֲבִיר **מֶמְשֶׁלֶת זָדוֹן** מִן הָאָרֶץ – "When You shall remove the **dominion of evil** from the earth." What is this "*Memsheles Zadon*" to which the prayer refers? Last week, we cited R' Yeruchem Olshin's explanation that it alludes to the Heavenly accusers, Celestial representatives of the nations of the earth. At this time, they join forces against Yisrael, aiming to persuade Hashem to reverse His selection of them as His Chosen People. We battle against them with prayer and ask Him instead that they be defeated.

R' YERUCHEM OFFERS AN ALTERNATIVE EXPLANATION, identifying the *Memsheles Zadon* as the general force of evil, which in most recent times seems to have had an astronomical rise. Underscoring the frightening surge we have witnessed in Satan's power on all fronts, he writes the following in his *sefer Yerach L'mo'adim* (*Yamim Nora'im* I, *ma'amar* 47, §7):

From Without and Within

KINDLY TAKE A MOMENT TO STUDY MISHNAS CHAYIM IN THE MERIT OF
YONAH BAS **SHMUEL** A"H
A FELLOW JEW WHO PASSED AWAY WITH NO RELATIVES TO ARRANGE TORAH STUDY ON BEHALF OF HER *NESHAMAH*

"The situation has deteriorated to such an extent that even a blind man can perceive how the dominance of the Memsheles Zadon has increased in the world. (This is apparent) from the hatred displayed by the 'seventy wolves' (nations of the world) against the 'lone sheep' that is Yisrael... as the former derive their power from the evil force of the Sitra Achra (Satan's dominion).

Sadly, it is even more (apparent) in the upsurge of ra (evil) that has made inroads even within our own communities. Specifically, (this is manifest) in the formidable power of defilement inherent in the impure devices that – through the rapid technological advances as of late – proliferate and develop further on a daily basis... (This has accelerated) to the point that there is accessible a device – the size of the palm of one's hand – which has the ability to destroy the Jewish soul, G-d forbid, and further its descent to the lowest abyss... And (this device) has produced many casualties.

All of this is a result of the upsurge of the force of impurity, which increases and escalates in front of our eyes. It leaves all astonished, with no one knowing what the next day will bring or when or how these tzaros will end... or how to prevent this horrific plague from spreading farther.

For this, we must increase and intensify our prayers and plead with our Father in Heaven to save us at the time of this terrifying war and 'remove the Memsheles Zadon from the land.' For there is no greater Memsheles Zadon than this."

The *sefer* containing these words – *Yerach L'mo'adim* – was published toward the end of 5774 (almost a year to the day of this writing). What is particularly alarming is how much more has occurred since then, and how much the above-mentioned situation has further degenerated in so short a time. Such is the case regarding the looming threats of both our physical and spiritual welfare.

Landmark Decisions?

IN THE INTERNATIONAL ARENA, THE PRESIDENT of the United States ended what had been a welcome respite – a tradition of friendliness toward the Jewish people. And he did so in a most nefarious and frightening way. Iran, a rogue nation across the globe, consistently and vocally calls for the annihilation of the Jews, who, in their words, are conveniently gathered in a small area. Thus, they refer to Eretz Yisrael as a "one-bomb country" (may Hashem protect us). And for reasons known only to him, the U.S. president felt it appropriate to make a deal with them, granting them legitimacy, billions of dollars and the license to produce a nuclear bomb.

And just when you might have thought the surrounding moral climate could not get much worse – it did. The "cause" for deviance has been championed for some time now; it has been discussed, lobbied for, celebrated, paraded, etc. But in an unprecedented move to bring the moral fiber of the country down yet another notch, these freakish relationships have been granted official recognition and enshrined into law. Thus, we have a situation where those who advocate decency and wholesomeness are derided and silenced, while those promoting perverseness are lauded and praised.

Indeed, it certainly seems reminiscent of the description of the state the world in the immediate pre-Messianic era, as Chazal describe in the Mishnah (*Sotah 9:15*):

> בְּעִקְבוֹת מְשִׁיחָא חֻצְפָּא יִסְגֵּא... הַמַּלְכוּת תֵּהָפֵךְ לְמִינוּת, וְאֵין תּוֹכֵחָה, בֵּית וַעַד יִהְיֶה לִזְנוּת... יִרְאֵי חֵטְא יִמָּאֵסוּ, וְהָאֱמֶת תְּהֵא נֶעְדֶּרֶת... פְּנֵי הַדּוֹר כִּפְנֵי הַכָּלֶב....

> "In the footsteps of Mashiach, chutzpah will increase... The government will turn to heresy, and none will protest; meeting places will be devoted to immorality... Those who fear sin will be despised;

truth will disappear... The face of the generation will resemble that of a dog..."

But this, in itself, is the silver lining. At the same time as matters seem to be spiraling ever downward and the *Memsheles Zadon* increases in power and scope, we are reminded that its end is near. In this regard, R' Yeruchem (*ibid. §8*) quotes the Chafetz Chaim, who reveals a most remarkable aspect about the nature of *ra*. Just as a candle flares up just before it is extinguished, and the night is darkest right before the crack of dawn, so does the power of the Sitra Achra surge right before its demise. As the Mishnah itself stated, such elements are the signs that Mashiach will soon arrive.

Based on all we have been only too shocked and saddened to witness – and armed with the knowledge of the Chafetz Chaim's message – perhaps our prayers will take on new meaning during these Days of Awe. The Mishnah also adds a positive and hopeful note: עַל מִי יֵשׁ לָנוּ לְהִשָּׁעֵן, עַל אָבִינוּ שֶׁבַּשָּׁמָיִם – "Upon whom can we rely? Upon our Father in Heaven." Let us then allow the words of the prayer to emanate, now more than ever, from the bottom of our hearts: וּבְכֵן תֵּן פַּחְדְּךָ ד' אֱלֹקֵינוּ עַל כֹּל מַעֲשֶׂיךָ... וְעוֹלָתָה תִּקְפָּץ פִּיהָ, וְכֹל הָרִשְׁעָה כֻּלָּהּ כְּעָשָׁן תִּכְלֶה, כִּי תַעֲבִיר מֶמְשֶׁלֶת זָדוֹן מִן הָאָרֶץ, וְתִמְלוֹךְ אַתָּה ד' לְבַדֶּךָ עַל כֹּל מַעֲשֶׂיךָ – "And so, place Your fear, Hashem our G-d, over all of Your creatures... And may the mouth of vice be closed, and all of the evil shall dissipate like smoke, when You remove the *Memsheles Zadon* from the earth. And may You, Hashem, reign alone over all of Your creations..."

לזכר ולעילוי נשמות

יעקב בן יהודה אריה ע"ה

ברײנדל בת ר' ברוך ע"ה

HA'AZINU

Tishrei: The Big Picture

IN COMPARISON TO THE REST OF THE YEAR, THERE seems to be almost an explosion of sorts in Tishrei – insofar as (Biblically mandated) *yamim tovim* are concerned. The winter is basically bereft of festivals. Pesach occurs in Nisan; a couple of months later, we encounter Shavuos. After this, again there is a respite. But then we arrive at Tishrei, and suddenly we have Rosh Hashanah, Yom Kippur and Sukkos in rapid succession.

THIS IS CERTAINLY NO HAPHAZARD ARRANGEMENT; as such, it must be that the three are somehow related. The **Connections** connection between Rosh Hashanah and Yom Kippur seems clear enough and indeed is outlined by Chazal. These are the Yamim Nora'im, the Days of Awe, with a judgment taking place on Rosh Hashanah and an opportunity extended until Yom Kippur to repent and reverse the ruling (*cf. Rosh Hashanah 16b*). But then, in short order, comes Sukkos, the "time of our rejoicing," replete with its unique *mitzvos*.

KINDLY TAKE A MOMENT TO STUDY MISHNAS CHAYIM IN THE MERIT OF
LEAH BAS AVROHOM A"H
A FELLOW JEW WHO PASSED AWAY WITH NO RELATIVES TO ARRANGE TORAH STUDY ON BEHALF OF HER *NESHAMAH*

How, exactly, does this festival fit in to the same scheme as the other Tishrei events?

Even when focusing on Sukkos on its own we are faced with certain perplexities. Of course, we are all familiar with the unique practices of the holiday – namely, the *mitzvos* of dwelling in a Sukkah and the taking of the four *minim* (species). But what do they have to do with each other? It doesn't seem plausible that they are random ordinances that happen to fall out at the same time of year. Furthermore, Sukkos is also marked, as stated above, as a time of supreme joy. This aspect becomes manifest in truly grand and public style, in the elaborate festivities of song, music and dancing at the *Simchas Beis Hasho'eivah* in the Beis Hamikdash.

Rosh Hashanah, Yom Kippur, and Sukkos. *Sukkah, lulav,* and mass merriment. Seemingly disparate elements, yet collected together in close proximity. It would be truly ideal if we could discover the seamless thread that connects them all.

That thread is provided by the Netziv.

The Conflict

IN THE LEAD-UP TO ROSH HASHANAH, WE CITED the Netziv's enlightening approach to the Yamim Nora'im. He explained that there are actually two matters that are adjudicated in Heaven at this time. The more familiar aspect is the judgment affecting individuals, in which Hashem assesses the standing of each and every person and determines his fate for the upcoming year.

But in addition to that, there is another peril hovering over the Jewish people at this time, one involving the nation as a whole. This is the attempt by the Celestial representatives of the nations of the earth to bring about the dissolution of Klal Yisrael. These Heavenly accusers gather together and seek to undo the status of Yisrael as the Chosen nation of Hashem. The Netziv demonstrates how the practices and prayers of the Yamim Nora'im period are aimed at defending Yisrael in the wake of this conflict, when their existence as a people is at stake.

This is actually a recurring theme in various places throughout the Netziv's Ha'amek Davar commentary on the Torah. He utilizes it to shed much light, as well, on the *yom tov* of Sukkos – for it also relates to this great Celestial battle. The war itself is waged during the Yamim Nora'im. And the outstanding question of who emerged victorious is clarified on Sukkos.

A Time to... Dance

THE NETZIV (*DEVARIM 16:15*) QUOTES A MOST illuminating *medrash* to this effect: "Two litigants appear before a judge; (when they emerge), how do we know who prevailed? The one who raises his spear (as a victory gesture)... Similarly, Yisrael and the nations enter in contention before Hashem on Rosh Hashanah, and we do not yet know who prevailed. But when Yisrael emerges... **bearing their *lulavim* and *esrogim***, we know that Yisrael are the victors."

But it is not only the taking of the four *minim* that serves as a gesture of victory; the Netziv (*Vayikra 23:43*) explains the mitzvah of dwelling in the sukkah in this light, as well. Such is the practice of a prevailing army; they demonstrate their victory by retaining the military formation of their encampment. The *sukkos* reflect this practice. "For I placed Yisrael in *sukkos* when I took them out from the land of Mitzrayim" (*ibid.*). This was a military arrangement, as "B'nei Yisrael were armed in departing from the land of Mitzrayim" (*Shemos 13:18*).

The celebratory nature of the festival is a further manifestation of this idea. In this respect, the Netziv puts forth a novel thought, one unbeknownst to many. He asserts that in addition to *lulav*, *sukkah*, and *simchah* (joy), there is yet another Biblical commandment pertaining to the festival: a mitzvah to dance. It is noteworthy that this was a hallmark of the grand *Simchas Beis Hasho'eivah* celebration in the Temple, as recorded in the Mishnah in Sukkah (*5:1,4*):

חֲסִידִים וְאַנְשֵׁי מַעֲשֶׂה הָיוּ מְרַקְּדִים לִפְנֵיהֶם בַּאֲבוּקוֹת שֶׁל אוֹר שֶׁבִּידֵיהֶן, וְאוֹמְרִים לִפְנֵיהֶן דִּבְרֵי שִׁירוֹת וְתִשְׁבָּחוֹת...

Ha'azinu / 209

> *"Pious people and men of deeds would dance before the people with fiery torches in their hands; they would emote before them words of song and praise..."*

This concept is derived from some apparently extraneous words in the Sukkos verses. After already issuing the command to be joyous on the holiday – *"V'samachta b'chagecha"* (*Devarim 16:14*) – the next *passuk* seems to repeat the directive: *"Tachog la'Hashem Elokecha* – 'Celebrate' before Hashem your G-d." Based on Chazal's teaching elsewhere (*cf. Chagigah 10b*), the Netziv defines the term of *"tachog"* here to refer specifically to the act of dancing: "You shall *dance* before Hashem." Additionally, since the issue of feeling joy was already addressed (in the previous *passuk*), the dancing directive must be based on a different calculation; i.e., it is not simply an expression of this joy, but functions as its own entity.

If the mitzvah to dance on Sukkos is not an outgrowth of the mitzvah of *simchah* – what is it then? The Netziv's explanation rounds out the underlying theme of all the Sukkos practices, and indeed, all of the Tishrei practices. For this dancing is also unique to the victorious party, demonstrating that, with Hashem's mercy, the Jews have once again prevailed over their enemies.

לזכר ולעילוי נשמת

ר' ניסן בן ר' שמואל ע"ה

Provide the powerful merit of Torah study and tefillah for the neshamah of your loved one.

Services

Mishnah and Gemara Study
An outstanding Torah scholar will complete a portion of *Mishnah* or *Gemara* on behalf of the *neshamah* of a loved one.

Kaddish Recital
A dedicated Torah scholar will recite Kaddish for the first eleven months after the passing of a loved one, as well as on the *yahrtzeit*.

Tehillim Recital
A serious Torah scholar will recite a portion of *Tehillim* on the day of the *yahrtzeit*.

Yizkor Recital
A dedicated Torah scholar will recite *Yizkor* on the proscribed holidays in memory of a loved one.

Publications

Nichum V'Nechamah: To Comfort and Be Comforted
An invaluable guide to the mitzvah of *nichum aveilim*, offering guidance and comfort to mourners and comforters. Includes special Woman to Woman subsection.
— Available in three separate formats: book, DVD, or MP3.

I Lost Someone Special
A remarkable, highly regarded picture book introducing young children to the concept of remaining linked to one who has passed away by earning *zechusim* on their behalf.

Aliyas Neshamah Curriculum
The highly acclaimed curriculum for teachers to present to children and teens about the concepts of the afterlife and how we can impact the souls of those who have passed on.

The Neshamah Should Have an Aliyah
A unique and innovative volume explaining the life-changing concept of providing merit for a soul and offering practical guidance for *aliyas neshamah* opportunities.
— Includes audiovisual CD with words of inspiration from world-renowned speakers Rabbi Yissocher Frand and Rabbi Paysach Krohn.

Prayers to Be Said at a Grave
Complete list of the most commonly recited prayers and psalms to be recited when visiting the cemetery, along with lucid instructions in English.

Support Group Handbook
An innovative handbook that includes the format and materials for effectively running a support group for those who have lost a parent.

TO ORDER ANY OF OUR SERVICES OR PUBLICATIONS,

Harness the incredible power of Torah study as a merit for:

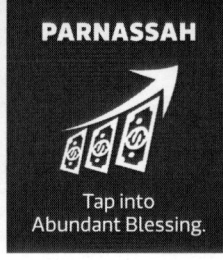

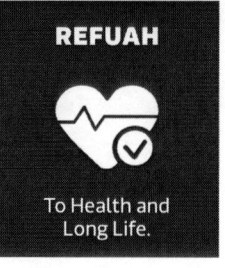

SHIDDUCHIM — Build a Beautiful Future.

ZERA KAYAMA — Follow the Road to Continuing a Chain.

PARNASSAH — Tap into Abundant Blessing.

REFUAH — To Health and Long Life.

We Offer

40 Days of Segulah
Imagine harnessing the power of Torah for 40 consecutive days!

Complete Masechta Segulah
Can you imagine finishing an entire *masechta* of Mishnah or Talmud? Can you imagine finishing the entire *Shas*? What tremendous *zechusim* this can bring to you and your family!

One Hour Vasikin Segulah
Many pious people arise early to pray precisely at the first ray of light, known as *vasikin*. The merit of Torah learning done directly before this time, between *chatzos halaylah* (midnight) and *vasikin*, is particularly powerful.

Unique Sefarim Segulah
There are other holy books, authored by extraordinarily pious individuals, which have been known to bring blessing and salvation to those who study them. Some of these volumes include *Zera Shimshon*, *Bas Ayin*, *Tomer Devorah*, *Kli Yakar*, *Ohr HaChayim*, *Alshich* and *Chafetz Chayim*.

Maseches Kinnim Segulah
The tractate of *Maseches Kinnim*, when learned with the commentary of the *Kan Mefureshes*, is especially beneficial for many *yeshuos*. The *tzaddeikes* Rebbetzin Batsheva Kanievsky, a"h, would often recommend this course of learning to people who sought her counsel in dealing with particular ailments.

PLEASE CONTACT: www.ChevrahLomdeiMishnah.org / (732) 364-7029

www.ChevrahLomdeiMishnah.org / (732) 364-7029

Made in United States
Cleveland, OH
19 February 2025